T0285960

RUSSIA IN FOUR CRIMINALS

For Edgar, and David and Jane

RUSSIA IN FOUR CRIMINALS

F E D E R I C O V A R E S E

polity

CENTRO
PER IL LIBRO
E LA LETTURA

Polity Press
65 Bridge Street
Cambridge CB2 1UR, UK

Polity Press
111 River Street
Hoboken, NJ 07030, USA

ISBN-13: 978-1-5095-6360-9

A catalogue record for this book is available from the British Library.

Library of Congress Control Number: 2024931020

Typeset in 12.5 on 15pt Dante
by Cheshire Typesetting Ltd, Cuddington, Cheshire

For further information on Polity, visit our website:
politybooks.com

CONTENTS

ACKNOWLEDGEMENTS

I am most grateful to Andrea Bosco, who encouraged me to write this book and provided most valuable guidance during its preparation for the Italian edition. Ian Malcolm enthusiastically embraced this new version for Polity. Roberto Esposito played a crucial role in supporting the publication of the English edition. My agents Marco Vigevani and Alberto Saibene championed the project from the start. In Italy, Maria Chiara Franceschelli cast her expert eye on an early version and suggested some corrections. Vania Facchinelli read several incarnations of the *Four Criminals*. I am most grateful to her. Barbara del Mercato and Roberto Roversi also offered valuable insights.

In Oxford, Elena Racheva helped me to locate innumerable sources and rectify several mistakes. Elena also provided valuable feedback at all stages of my work. Without her help, this book would be much poorer indeed. I greatly benefitted from a special session of my Oxford University CRIMGOV research group. Alae Baha, Zora Hauser, Eva Stambøl and Emilia Ziosi were present and subjected the text to a barrage of most welcome and useful criticism. My Oxford colleagues Hannah Brawn and Tim Davies were kind enough to read and comment. Judith Pallot has given me detailed comments on all chapters, and I hope I have managed to rectify several errors. Mauro Vignati has shared his deep knowledge of cybercrime with me. Sergei Guriev and Stathis Kalyvas have encouraged me to pursue this style of writing.

The three institutions I was affiliated to while working on this book gave me enough time and peace to conclude the research. They are the Department of Sociology and Nuffield College at Oxford University, and le Centre d'études européennes et de politique compare at Sciences Po, Paris.

During a trip to Lviv in April 2022, I had the privilege of discussing some themes of the book with Yaroslav Hrytsak and Maria Tomak, to whom I extend my sincere thanks for their company and assistance.

Two chapters, in different versions, were published in the Italian daily *la Repubblica*. I am grateful to the editor, Maurizio Molinari, and the deputy editor, Carlo Bonini, for their trust.

While writing *Russia in Four Criminals*, I deeply felt the absence of David and Jane Cornwell's kindness and encouragement. I miss them very much. This book is dedicated to their memory, and to my son, Edgar Varese, who embodies virtues that stand in stark contrast with those of the characters described in this book.

Oxford, Paris, Ferrara
24 December 2023

A NOTE TO THE READER

Russian is among a handful of languages in the world that lack a universally recognized system of transliteration into English. When spelling names and words, I adhere to the British Standards Institution (BSI) model, which most closely approximates Russian pronunciation. I depart from it only for the names of some well-known figures – for example Berezovsky, Dzerzhinsky, Yeltsin, and Navalny (and not Berezovskii, Dzerzhinskii, El'tsin, Naval'nyi) – and for a few very popular names of persons, such as Olga (and not Ol'ga), or places, such as Perm (and not Perm'). Despite my best efforts, I am sure that inconsistencies remain.

In the hope of making the reading of this book flow smoothly, I have chosen to forgo the traditional format of numbered footnotes. Instead, I list all the references in a Notes and References chapter, linking each bibliographic item directly to the relevant passage and supplying the page number and the linear context of the citation. For example, an entry of the form

> 5 **predictability and equality** See Stephen Holmes, 'Lineages of the Rule of Law', in Adam Przeworski and José María Maravall (eds.), *Democracy and the Rule of Law* (Cambridge University Press, Cambridge 2003), p. 20.

is a reference to Holmes' article for the discussion of predictability and equality at page 5 in this book. This approach, inspired by Timothy Snyder's *The Road to Unfreedom* (Bodley Head, London 2018), achieves the goal of traditional footnotes while being inconspicuous. It also allows for an in-depth exploration of the topics discussed in the text. As usual, each source is cited in full the first time and by short title afterwards.

Unfortunately, this is not a book of fiction. The characters discussed in these pages are real and the stories factual.

GLOSSARY

Key Russian acronyms and expressions:

FSB	Federal Security Service (1995–)
Gulag	Chief Administration of Corrective Labour Camps*
KGB	Committee for State Security (1954–91)
Komsomol	Young Communist League (1918–91)
MVD	Ministry of Internal Affairs
progon	a collective letter written by the community of the *vory-v-zakone*
vory-v-zakone	thieves in law, i.e. criminals professing the code

Key cybercrime terms:

bulletproof hosting	web hosting or server hosting services provided by companies or individuals for content that is mostly illegal
cybercrime-as-a-service and (CaaS)	a model in which cybercriminals offer various hacking or cybercriminal tools services to other individuals or groups for a fee
money mules	in cybercrime, individuals who assist in the transfer of illegally obtained funds or assets

private bulletin boards or Bulletin Board Systems (BBS)	computer systems that served as online meeting places before the widespread use of the internet; they were operated over telephone lines through modems
ransomware	a type of malicious software that encrypts a victim's files or locks them out of their computer or network

* This acronym, which originally referred only to a division of the Soviet secret police that ran the forced labour camps from the 1930s until the early 1950s, is generally used to designate the entire system of forced labour camps in the Soviet Union.

INTRODUCTION

When I arrived in the city of Perm in the Ural region in 1994, I went to live in a students' hostel. It was certainly not for the first time in my life. I had lived in undergraduate rooms at the University of Bologna, where the main activities were staying up all night, smoking and organizing the next meeting of the student collective, and in Oxbridge colleges, where political discussions took place in colleges across high table seats reserved for graduate students. In the dormitory in Perm, no one talked about politics and no one seemed to spend any time sweating over books. It was a typical Soviet-style building, not far from the station: a flat-fronted white block with ten floors and a canteen near the entrance. I was one of the very few guests on my floor, even though there were a great many comings and goings of all kinds of people, some in suits, some in sports outfits, some in jeans and leather jackets. When I peeked behind the doors of the other rooms, I saw piles of goods. The student residence seemed to be a microcosm of what the country had become: a large warehouse in the post-Soviet bazaar. Everything was for sale, everyone was doing something other than their official role, everything was *biznes*.

Those who were supposed to live on the same floor as me simply sublet their rooms to what appeared to be a well-organized gang. After a few days I got to speak to the boss, who went by the English name of George. He was curious to meet me. He must have been in his twenties and had bristly hair, a face marked by untreated acne, and an outward bullish demeanour. Once I got to know him, he turned out to be an intelligent lad and a hard worker of humble origins. He invited me to his 'office' at the other end of the corridor. The scene left me stunned. On a wooden table was a calculator and several notebooks with beautifully handwritten numbers and names, while the rest of the space was occupied by dozens of boxes, the kind used for reams of paper. But there was no photocopier: those boxes were full of money, mostly in foreign denominations.

The gang was doing pretty well, I thought, even though I did not see much security. I soon realized I wasn't looking at the profits of a Russian mini drug cartel or prostitution racket. George and his friends traded in money, ran a rudimentary commodity exchange, and engaged in the occasional money-lending operation. At that time inflation was around 15 per cent per month. This was 1994, the year of Black Tuesday, when the value of the US dollar went from 3,081 to 3,926 roubles on 11 October: in a matter of hours some became very rich, while many were left very poor. In a few years Russians came face to face with the concepts of 'purchasing power' and 'hyperinflation'. Both became a very real part of everyday life. In 1992 the young economists hired by Yeltsin to dismantle the Soviet economic system decided to liberalize prices, and the savings of Russian families immediately vaporized, generating a demand for stable currency.

George coordinated a complex network of people who had currency (especially dollars and German marks) and were looking for clients. The money often came from the banking system: corrupt officials passed on to George dollars at bargain prices, for a small fee under the table. At one time a company that sold timber on the international market urgently needed to convert $45,000 into roubles, to pay suppliers. George spent several nights on the phone to raise the funds. On other occasions the currency was provided by foreigners who were passing through and by people returning from abroad. Still others shuttled between Perm and Moscow, where they bought dollars and sold them back to George. George had to make sure that he was paid in a timely fashion, so he wouldn't hold on to the roubles for too long. All transactions took place in cash and were based on trust; no official contract was signed.

When the news spread that an 'English' student had arrived, for a moment I became the centre of attention. The quid pro quo was simple: they would tell me how the nascent Russian capitalism worked, and I would give them my British pounds. In any case, George offered much better rates than the bank around the corner, which went bankrupt two months after my arrival.

'My word is gold', mused George, a line I imagined he'd heard on some television series or read in a *Capitalism for Dummies* book. I could at last observe with my own eyes the mythical (to me) 'informal economy'. It was difficult to tell whether these trades were illegal. Legislation was constantly changing, and the boundary between what was lawful and what was not seemed to have disappeared. At the same time, those who had nothing could become very

rich, the old constraints had disappeared, and the relationship between efforts and results had evaporated. George's
commerce was profitable largely because it took place in
the shadow of a parasitic state, which allowed the young
people's gang in my student hall to exist.

Yet something was missing. How could George be certain that he was being paid on time? Was the word of his
clients enough? And who made sure that George wasn't
robbed? As the weeks went by, I noticed some changes.
At first, the rooms' doors were refitted with reinforced
iron locks. Then armed guards began stationing in the cor-
ridors. One night there was a fight outside my room.

In the meantime I had started to date a young Russian
woman who was spending many nights with me. I had the
feeling that it would have been better, for the safety of both,
to move out and find another place; so we went to live in an
apartment owned by friends. As time went by, I heard that
two 'mafias' had taken an interest in George's *biznes*. One
was made up of former KGB officials and veterans of the
war in Afghanistan, the other by former prisoners freshly
released, who followed the traditional rules of the criminal
world. I was not witnessing the spontaneous emergence of
a peaceful extra-legal order free from the traps of the Soviet
Union, a self-regulating free market where the best business
ideas would inevitably succeed. Success was a function of
access to violence, which was everywhere. Western newspapers ran headlines such as 'The Wild East', and Moscow
was compared to 1920s' Chicago. Trust is a great thing, but
unfortunately it was in short supply. George was about to
get into serious trouble. I would learn about his fate only at
the end of my research trip.

The question I ask in this book is simple: has Russia ever
emerged from the political and economic quandaries of

the 1990s? Has there ever been a fair guarantor of people's rights since I met George in a student hostel in provincial Russia in 1994? This is a big question. By finding an answer, we can say something important about the relationship between the rule of law and democracy, with Russia as a fitting case study. The rule of law is predicated on two principles: predictability and equality. Laws should be codified and applied equally to all people in the same situation (or at least a political system based on the rule of law must do its best to approximate this ideal). Democracy is ultimately a system of rules that strives to represent and protect all people, equally. If a class of citizens are routinely not protected, or if a person who is protected today can become the victim of the system tomorrow, then we have lawlessness and we live in a world governed by unpredictable diktats. As noted by the German philosopher Jürgen Habermas, 'there is a conceptual relation – and not simply an historically accidental relation – between law and democracy'. Surely Russia has changed dramatically since the 1990s, and crime has declined; but has it ever been able to provide equality and predictability, hence has it ever embarked on the road to democracy?

There are several ways of venturing an answer. I decided to tackle the question by following the lives and tribulations of four characters who exemplify different moments along this trajectory. Vyacheslav Ivan'kov (chapter 1) began his criminal career in the latter part of the Khrushchev Thaw (1960s), when most of his peers spent their lives behind bars. In prison they developed a secret jargon and an initiation ritual, and their bodies were covered in tattoos. The sect to which they belonged was known as 'thieves in law', an expression that refers to professional criminals who follow a code of honour ('the law'). Ivan'kov would become the most feared and the best known representative of this fraternity. His move to New York in 1992 ensured that his fame became global (he featured on the cover of *Time* magazine). Ivan'kov's main activities were settling disputes among entrepreneurs who could not turn to the state, retrieving stolen goods, and dispensing a very peculiar form of justice. Gorbachev's reforms in the 1980s had failed to equip the market economy with provisions that allow for fair exchanges to take place. A figure like Ivan'kov is what was missing from George's business model back in Perm: a protector who ensured that nobody got robbed.

During the 1990s, many observers believed that Yeltsin was going to inject a degree of certainty and fairness into society, the state acting as an honest broker with the interest of the people at heart. Then democracy and the market would finally arrive in Russia, the argument went. Yeltsin made things worse. Privatization was for him a means of taking away resources from the 'red' managers and giving them to a trusted group of entrepreneurs and political supporters. He had no interest in creating an independent judiciary. Political opponents were persecuted; this process culminated in the bombing of the freely elected parliament in 1993, the adoption of an authoritarian constitution in 1994, and the Second Chechen War in 1999. A crucial ally of Yeltsin in those years was an unscrupulous entrepreneur, the most emblematic one of his generation: Boris Berezovsky (chapter 2), who began his career with a joint venture with an Italian company.

Berezovsky, before he committed suicide in 2013 in a villa in the English countryside not far from where I live today, made his fortune through scams and lies. He was no different from George's customers back in Perm, who promised to pay and instead ran away with the money, using raw violence in the process. The supreme organ of the state, the president, instead of punishing Berezovsky, rewarded him with privileged access to the privatization of assets. The lesson was clear for all to see: every form of illegality is allowed, as long as you pay back those in power. I met him briefly in the extravagantly furnished club he had created in Moscow, the Logovaz House, where scantily clad women mingled with elderly statesmen and businesspeople. Parties started late in the evening, so it was best to get invited for a meeting after 8 p.m.

Berezovsky was instrumental in ensuring Putin's election to the presidency in 2000, on the back of a criminal war against Chechnya (an integral part of the Russian Federation) that had been fuelled by a series of horrific terrorist attacks against ordinary Russians in 1999. Many suspect that those bombings were engineered by the very authorities supposed to protect the people. In any case, Putin won the elections and continued his predecessor's project of crashing the democracy and ensuring that his allies controlled the economy. After he liquidated most Yeltsin-era entrepreneurs and opposition politicians, Putin began to turn on the criminal underworld. Starting in 2014, dissidents and lawbreakers who did not comply with the diktats of the prison administration were raped and tortured with impunity. We know these facts thanks to Sergei Savel'ev (chapter 3): arrested for drug dealing, Sergei was a computer expert assigned to the Saratov Prison Infirmary, where he managed the workstations of a dozen facilities. He was then given the task of downloading the torture videos and distributing them to a few trusted officials. Faced with the horror of the images he saw, he decided to copy them and, once released, he smuggled the footage into the West. The videos were published on the website of a Franco-Russian NGO in November 2021. Sergei was able to prove that the state had condoned and indeed encouraged the mass rape of convicts. I spoke to him extensively in 2021, and again in March 2022.

In the meantime Russia has become a cybercrime paradise, alongside countries such as Brazil, Nigeria, and Vietnam. The story of Nikita Kuzmin (chapter 4) shows how the Putin regime has clay feet: it must come to terms with a criminality that it does not control. Nikita Kuzmin, the inventor of the world's most powerful computer virus, Gozi, is an emblematic personality in this secretive world. He is the adopted son of a well-known singer and was briefly jailed in the US for his crimes and retained the same lawyer as Donald Trump's son. Russian hackers such as Nikita operate in relative autonomy, but must follow rules: they cannot attack targets within the Russian Federation and, when asked, must assist the state in its cyberwar against the West. This is why they are allowed to operate with impunity.

In the Conclusions I link the micro stories with the macro picture of the post-Soviet period. The four stories told in this book teach us that the golden age of post-Soviet democracy and rule of law was very short, if it ever really existed. Indeed, a saying I often heard in the late 1980s in the Soviet Union was 'strike the iron while Gorbachev is here' – a variant of 'strike the iron while it is hot': in other words, take advantage of freedom of speech and economic liberty before Gorbachev is removed. The end of Russia's freedom happened much sooner than most people think. The state was never a fair enforcer of contracts. If anything, this job was done by the likes of Ivan'kov in the informal economy. The choice for the many Georges that sprung up in the 1990s was to seek either mafia protection or political

protection. The criminal war in Ukraine is a direct conse-
quence of the fear of democracy among the political elite.
The West was not an innocent bystander: it trusted Yeltsin
and his circle of unscrupulous men and women, allowing
them to hide their money in western banks without realiz-
ing that Yeltsin was the prelude to Putin. Now we all suffer
the consequences.

Towards the end of my stay in Perm I was told that,
within a year, George lost everything and fell victim to a
loan shark, who tortured him and chained him to a radia-
tor for a month. He never recovered from the experience
and is now cared for by his elderly parents. That nice and
daring boy, whom I met in a student hostel when we were
both young, is gone. He is just another victim of a god that
failed.

CHAPTER 1

THE MAFIA BOSS
VYACHESLAV IVAN'KOV

The only time I came face to face with Vyacheslav K. Ivan'kov was when he was dead. On my last trip to Russia in 2017, I headed to the cemetery where he is buried (as I narrate in my book *Mafia Life*). In Moscow there is a hierarchy of death. Behind Lenin's Mausoleum there is a small cemetery where twelve leaders of the Communist Party and the Revolution are buried, including Stalin, Dzerzhinsky, Brezhnev, Chernenko, and Andropov.

The second most important cemetery in Moscow is Novodevich'e, where the graves of Chekhov, Gorbachev's wife, and Yeltsin can be found. The third cemetery is called Vagan'kovskoye; it is located a few metro stops away from the centre, near a convent of the same name. It is a resting place for lesser-known celebrities, who were nonetheless an integral part of the country's elite. Ordinary people would never be admitted. Near the entrance stands the imposing funerary monument of the man who coached the Russian national hockey team in the 1980s and 1990s.

After navigating the maze of graves with some difficulty, I hired a guide who led me to plot 26. There lies Ivan'kov, buried next to his mother. A life-size sculpture portrays him in an informal pose, seated, hands in his pockets, the glimpse of a gold chain disappearing into his semi-open shirt. Behind the statue lie two black marble steles. One reproduces a traditional Russian icon, Madonna and child, designed to symbolize the deceased's religiosity (he was famous for his collection of ancient icons). The second stele depicts the bars of a cell overlooking an empty landscape. The heroes of the Soviet Union who rest near Ivan'kov are celebrated with objects related to their professions, for example the silhouette of a tank for a general, or that of an aeroplane for a jet fighter. For Ivan'kov, that item is the prison.

In the light of this monument, we can conclude that Ivan'kov had a successful life. Until he died in 2009, he was considered the most important mobster in the post-Soviet world. Born in Moscow on 2 January 1940, he was the son of an unemployed, alcoholic, and abusive father, who soon abandoned the family. His mother suffered from a particular mental illness, mysophobia – fear of dirt and contamination – which pushed her to wash objects obsessively, for instance dishes and the floor. Ivan'kov was a rather weak child, beset by various ailments. But he was passionate about freestyle wrestling and judo, and these two sports helped him fend neighbourhood bullies off.

Around the age of fourteen he enrolled in the State School of Circus Arts, but was forced to abandon it after a disastrous fall from the trapeze that resulted in a severe concussion. Shortly afterwards, Ivan'kov was involved in a car accident. The combination of these misfortunes appears to be the cause of several mental disorders, such as schizophrenia. Yet we may want to exercise a degree of caution over this diagnosis: it is unlikely that a fall from a trapeze could cause such a disease. In the Soviet Union, it was common practice to bribe a doctor to certify someone as schizophrenic, especially to keep that person out of the army. In any case, the Soviet healthcare system recognized him as permanently disabled, a status he would use multiple times to avoid prison. After school he took on various odd jobs: mechanic in an industrial plant, assistant in a photo lab, coach in a physical education school, and blacksmith.

During this period, Ivan'kov had to support not only his mother but also his family. In 1960 he married Lidiya Aivazova, with whom he had two children. This marked the beginning of his new profession as a thief and pickpocket. Arrested for the first time in 1965, he managed to avoid prison thanks to a diagnosis of schizophrenia and was sent to a psychiatric hospital.

Towards the end of the 1960s he joined a gang of around thirty members led by Gennady 'the Mongol' Korkov. During this period he was already known by the nickname Yaponchik, 'the Little Japanese', on account of his almond-shaped eyes. At the time of the Thaw (the period when the Soviet Union relaxed its repressive policies after the death of Stalin in 1953), the black market was growing exponentially, because the system was unable to produce consumer goods and efficient services. The Mongol's group specialized in extorting money from corrupt managers and small entrepreneurs who, by definition, could not turn to the state. Korkov was infamous for his violent methods: victims were taken to a forest and forced to dig their own graves. He also hired a torture master, whose nickname has gone down into history as 'the 'Executioner' because he perfected the sawing technique: those who didn't yield to extortion demands were placed in a coffin, the lid was closed, and the Executioner began sawing the wood. I wonder whether this idea had not been suggested by Ivan'kov himself, who had worked in a circus. Another member of the group was 'the Bituminist', who specialized in pouring hot tar on the victims. Ivan'kov's recognized contribution was the suggestion that group members disguise themselves as police officers, to make the victims open the door and get robbed. The gang was active for about five years before being crushed by the police in 1972. The only one to avoid arrest was the Little Japanese.

After his apprenticeship with the Mongol, Ivan'kov was ready to establish his own gang. His operational principles were similar to those he had learned from his mentor, primarily the ruthless use of violence. 'Killing is as easy as lighting a cigarette', he said. It is rumoured that he buried a restaurant owner alive and poured cement over the coffin. He continued dealing with black market entrepreneurs, but introduced a crucial innovation: he told his men to stop robbing wealthy speculators. Instead, it was much more profitable to offer them protection. If businesspeople were robbed, Ivan'kov's men would mobilize to recover the goods; if they owed a debt, Ivan'kov's men would collect it. For example, in 1981, a renowned stamp collector named Arkadii Nisenzon took possession of several icons that did not belong to him. The 'legitimate' owners (who themselves had no official ownership title) turned to Ivan'kov to either recover the stolen items or obtain compensation. Posing as a collector himself, Ivan'kov made an appointment with Nisenzon. At the meeting, he demanded 100,000 roubles – 60,000 for the stolen icons and 40,000 as compensation for the theft – an astronomical amount at the time (the average gross salary in those years was about 235 roubles). Ivan'kov, of course, used strong-arm tactics: the collector was beaten severely and threatened to be dissolved in acid. Only then did Nisenzon agree to pay, after which he was released. Ivan'kov's gang was thus a proto-mafia, providing criminal protection to wealthy and powerful individuals who could not use legal avenues to assert their demands. Business was booming with assignments to be undertaken in various cities of the Soviet Union, from Riga to Kazan to Sverdlovsk.

In March 1974 the doors of Soviet prisons finally opened to the Little Japanese. He became involved in a brawl in a restaurant on the outskirts of Moscow. A group of Georgian criminals insulted his girlfriend, an affront that questioned the leader's authority, so he had to react not so much out of respect for the woman, but to defend his reputation. Instead of using physical force, Ivan'kov and his henchmen pulled out guns. This led to a shoot-out in a public place, an unheard-of event in the Soviet Union of the 1970s. Two bullets ended up in the body of a Georgian who miraculously survived. Ivan'kov managed to avoid conviction for attempted murder, but was found guilty of possessing a fake passport (discovered during a search of his apartment) and was sentenced to seven months and fifteen days in prison. The period that Ivan'kov spent in Butyrka, an infamous prison in the Tverskoi District in central Moscow, nevertheless marked a turning point in his criminal career. It was there that he became part of the caste of the country's most powerful criminals: the thieves in law.

In the Soviet Union a complex criminal underworld existed. At its apex was a brotherhood of leaders known as *vory v zakone*. This expression can be translated as 'criminals who obey a code of honour', but it is often rendered, more literally, as 'thieves in law'. The brotherhood traces its origins to nineteenth-century guilds of common criminals. Political prisoners confined to the Gulag during the Soviet era encountered some of its members and described their behaviour. In the 1940s and 1950s, they wore rudimentary aluminium crosses around their necks and often had long beards. Their bodies were covered in tattoos. A French citizen convicted as a spy by the Soviets after the Second World War saw them up close. In his memoirs, he recounts that they had on their chests 'an image of angels praying on either side of a crucifix; below were the phrases "Lord, save your servant!" or "I believe in God"', which attest to a deep connection with religion.

The *vory* spoke a language of their own, with a Russian grammatical structure but a distinct vocabulary. They continually challenged Soviet power while remaining faithful to their own morality. Despite breaking the law, they were organized in groups that had rules and customs of their own, a language, and a rudimentary division of labour and extended across different regions. The Second World War created a serious fracture in the brotherhood, between those who had agreed to join a military unit formed by Gulag prisoners and the 'honest' *vory* – those who had refused to serve the country during the war, thus respecting the dictates of the code of honour, which prohibited any act of submission to the Soviet state (a similar split is underway today, around the 2022 conflict in Ukraine). The brotherhood was almost completely wiped out in the 1950s. Those who survived internal struggles and state repression continued to respect the code and, with the relaxation of the prison regime in the 1960s and 1970s, managed to recruit new members. One of them was Ivan'kov.

The initiation ritual, also known as 'baptism' or 'coronation', marks the formal entry into the brotherhood. According to the rules, one must be proposed by two sponsors, who in Ivan'kov's case were Valerii Kuchuloriya, known as Piso, and Gaik Gevorkyan, known as Goga Erevanskii. During the ritual, Piso spoke first, proposing the recruit's affiliation, praising his criminal career, and listing his successes in the underworld. The criminal assembly concluded that Ivan'kov was devoted to the traditions of the *vory*, could guide other criminals and pass judgement justly and fairly, would use his authority effectively, and was able to gather resources to feed the common Russian mafia fund. A crucial criterion for admission was that the future *vor* had no ties to law enforcement and had never worked for a state institution. It is not clear how 'the Commission' judged the odd jobs undertaken by the Little Japanese in his youth. As in all mafias, general principles are always adapted to power dynamics, and Ivan'kov had many affiliates who wanted him in the organization.

The elders were satisfied with his background, and Ivan'kov could swear allegiance to the criminal world. Immediately after the oath, the oldest *vor* listed the organization's rules.

Avoid any conflict with fellow *vory* and do not undermine their authority. Respect the rulings of *vory* courts and work hard to collect funds for the brotherhood. Never work for the state or join the army, pay taxes, or take a job in the prison administration. You can take a wife, but the brotherhood comes before anything else. Passive homosexuality is strictly forbidden. Once you're in the *vory*, you can never leave!

Through informal channels, news of Ivan'kov's 'corona-tion' spread throughout the criminal world, ensuring that friends and enemies alike were aware of it.

At that point Ivan'kov was allowed to have the symbol of his new status tattooed on his body. It was a pain-ful process, during which the design was traced onto the skin using a needle and a razor. Ivan'kov chose the eight-pointed star. This symbol has immense significance across different religions and cultures. It appears to origi-nate in ancient Mesopotamia and symbolizes the moon, the sun, the planets, the stars, and the comets. In ancient times it was the emblem of the goddess Ishtar, who held sway over love, fertility, and warfare. The *vory* must have borrowed it from Orthodox Christianity, for which the number eight signifies resurgence and resurrection. When tattooed on the skin, the star marks a criminal born anew in the brotherhood. Depending on where it is imprinted on one's body, the image has a different meaning. If it appears on the knees, it means that the *vor* is worthy of respect and will never kneel before anyone. When the image is drawn on the chest, it means that the person is one of the most respected criminals, the elite of the elite. Anyone wearing that tattoo without earning it risks his life. Ivan'kov adorned himself with two stars tattooed on his chest, one on his right shoulder and another on the left. For this reason, many sources have referred to him as the head of the Russian mafia. While the *vory* did not 'anoint' any single figure as their head, Ivan'kov undoubt-edly towered over this clandestine world for the best part of forty years.

He was keen to present himself as devoted to the principles of thieves in law, above all to the rejection of riches.

I hate luxury. I don't need wealth, diamonds, private planes, yachts, and other nonsense. I lead a semi-spartan lifestyle. I'll have everything I need, but I repeat: I don't need anything! I have completely different values, spiritual values. I've endured too much in life. I haven't even eaten white bread. For me, the dawn is more valuable than for someone – a billion dollars... I'd rather gnaw on cobblestones and feel like a decent person than eat oysters splashed in champagne and feel like a complete shit.

Despite his professed distance from the Soviet power structures, Ivan'kov always managed to stay one step ahead of the militia, which was notoriously corrupt. This was the case for instance in 1975, when he tried to collect a debt from an entrepreneur who had in the meantime become an informant. The police set up a trap to catch him red-handed, but Ivan'kov was warned and did not show up for the appointment. Undoubtedly he had important friends for whom he did favours and solved problems, like a classic mafioso.

When he was finally arrested for the extortion of the stamp collector in 1981, Ivan'kov could rely on top-notch defence. His lawyer told a Russian newspaper that 'very powerful and important people' asked him to take the case on. He added:

Ivan'kov had a strong personality. They told me that I would meet a very important boss, a 'godfather'; so I expected him to be a bit different. Instead, a slim man arrived, in good shape, dressed very well, with a blazer and a handkerchief in the pocket, neatly combed. I was particularly struck by his eyes: small, piercing. It seemed like he wanted to cut through a person with his gaze. He

was also very tough and rude, but at the same time intelligent, with a strategic mind and an unyielding will. It's
almost impossible to break him.

When the lawyer asked if he intended to confess, Ivan'kov
replied: 'No. Even if they hang me upside down on hooks.'
The lawyer thought it wasn't empty bravado.

Even with a high-profile lawyer, in April 1982 Ivan'kov
received a fourteen-year sentence and imprisonment in
a maximum-security facility. He was sent to Talaya in
the Magadan region, in the Russian Far East. Life behind
bars was not easy for thieves in law. Both the authorities
and the other criminals were eager to see him make a
mistake. According to the informal yet rigid rules of the
prison, those who come into contact with the caste of the
untouchables become part of it and can be harassed with
impunity. Ivan'kov was forced to share a cell with a prisoner convicted of rape and hence classified as untouchable.
It is unclear whether Ivan'kov managed to fend off the
assaults from his cellmate, but we know that the man was
soon attacked and died.

Transferred to another penal institution, in Tulun, the
Little Japanese continued to act as a mediator among
inmates. As an authoritative *vor*, he also dealt with the
prison administration on behalf of the fraternity and other
inmates. He would solve problems and defuse conflicts.
Such a function did not equate to working for the authorities (that was prohibited by the code). A fellow thief in law
who was in the same prison recounted the following: 'He
solved problems that were too thorny for the authorities to
tackle.' Often the prison leadership 'was forced to bow to
the Little Japanese'. For example, he managed to find coal
when the money ran out and to avert a potential violent

confrontation between guards and inmates. Yet he also found himself in conflict with the local mafia chief, the Georgian thief in law Makho (Il'ya Simoniya). Ivan'kov rejected Makho's authority, deeming him unfit to rule over the Irkutsk region. According to him, Makho's claim to the title of thief in law was unjustified, given his past association with the Komsomol – the youth wing of the Communist Party in the Soviet Union. Thus Ivan'kov initiated a campaign among influential *vory* to strip Makho of his status. In retaliation, Makho circulated rumours that portrayed the Little Japanese as a KGB informant. To quell the whispers, Ivan'kov orchestrated an attack on a guard. The episode resulted in severe injuries and the guard's subsequent transfer.

In essence, Ivan'kov was far from being an exemplary prisoner, having transgressed regulations on twenty-six occasions and having been subjected to solitary confinement at least sixteen times (if not thirty-six, as other accounts would have it). Havin been put through two trials and given additional sentences, he appeared an unlikely candidate for early release on the basis of good behaviour, and was slated to remain in jail until the mid-1990s. But influential allies intervened on his behalf, among them a prominent Soviet-era singer and a future 1996 presidential candidate with vested interests in Moscow hotels. The two spearheaded a petition for Ivan'kov's release that proved successful: it prompted the Supreme Court of the Russian Federation to overturn the sentence for health reasons. In 1991 Ivan'kov was a free man.

The Russia of 1991 was very different from that of 1981. Western cafés, expensive restaurants, and trendy nightclubs had sprung up everywhere, in Moscow and other cities. The new ruling class wore Rolex watches, Italian shoes, and gold bracelets and had a new and fancy item, the mobile phone. Women were dressed in Versace outfits and carried Ferragamo bags. Prostitution was rampant. Luxury was unrestrained. In those years I loved to visit new clubs. Entering was like taking a historical and geographical leap: after passing through the typical Soviet entrance, often in monumental concrete or marble style, I found myself in the likes of Studio 54 in New York. My favourite club was Arlechino (*sic*). It was located inside a stone and aluminium building in modernist Soviet style, built by the architect Vladimir Ginzburg in the 1980s, in clear contrast to the classical style of the Krasnopresnenskaya metro station right in front of it. In 1989 it became the headquarters of Soviet Union's *cinémathèque*, Moscow's answer to La Cinémathèque française at 51 Rue de Bercy in Paris. The cinemas inside were the first to install the Dolby Stereo system in the Soviet Union and were a must-see for cinephiles like me. In 1991 an Italian restaurant opened in the foyer. The administrators then had a brilliant idea: they removed the chairs in the evening – and the film halls turned into dance floors, with American and European DJs. In 1995 even Naomi Campbell made an appearance. The profits were exorbitant, as was the entrance fee. Soon Arlechino became the favourite club of the new gangs, which fought – and not metaphorically – for control over Russia's economic jewels. At least ten people were killed for control over the venue. One of them was the architect Ginzburg himself, who thus simply became another victim of those years, for no apparent reason.

Behind the glamour of the 1990s there was indeed an exponential growth of violence. Initially, Gorbachev's liberal policies had led to the release of many prisoners. Some had been victims of the regime, but many others were professional criminals. The Soviet leader proclaimed the end of state monopoly on the economy, and this gave rise to the cooperative movement (the Law of Cooperatives); but he did not consider that an effective market economy requires a system to resolve disputes among producers through courts and civil law norms. Finally, he decided to launch a campaign against vodka consumption in order to reduce endemic alcoholism. Consumption was not prohibited, but the bottles produced by state-owned companies were few and very expensive. Almost immediately, a thriving black market emerged: vodka was produced clandestinely in factories, industrial facilities, and homes, often using perfume, glass-cleaning material, and shoe polish; and every year thousands of Russians died as a result of drinking adulterated vodka. The chaotic privatization and price liberalization under Yeltsin did the rest, destroying the value of the rouble and making all state officials poor overnight; police officers began selling themselves to the highest bidder. This is how Russia became a 'crime superpower', as the president himself was forced to admit in a 1994 speech.

In the early 1990s, the old-style *vory*, with years of prison behind them and their bodies covered in tattoos, had to face new and formidable enemies. Criminals from Chechnya arrived in Moscow in the late 1980s and began running extortion rackets against the first entrepreneurs who had organized themselves into cooperatives. Soon the Chechens specialized in the sale of used cars (in fact they controlled an open-air market at the South River Terminal in Moscow – and also car dealerships). Those were the years when every heinous crime was attributed to Chechen gangs, which, by some estimates, were a thousand members strong in Moscow alone. This new mafia did not adhere to the rules of traditional thieves in law. It was composed of very closed clans that spoke a foreign language.

The Chechen Republic itself, formally part of the Russian Federation, was effectively a separate state, in which Russian authorities had no investigative power, and had become an international trading hub for heroin. Apart from Chechens, there were also Azerbaijani gangs vying for control over the drug trade. But the most violent battles were fought to conquer hotels, banks, and nightclubs such as the Arlechino. In addition to Chechens, Azerbaijanis, and old-style *vory* like Ivan'kov, there were also unemployed athletes (especially boxers) and soldiers who had fought in Afghanistan or served in Germany, ready to be recruited or to form their own group. According to the Russian Ministry of Internal Affairs, in 1993 there were about 3,000 organized criminal groups in Russia.

New opportunities, people trained in violence trying to get a piece of the bonanza, and a weak state: these made the Great Mob War of the early 1990s possible. According to the Ministry of Internal Affairs, there were 100 contract killings in 1992, and the number rose to 250 the following year. In 1994 the number of contract killings reached 500. Homicides per 100,000 people increased from 9.8 in 1988 to 32.4 in 1994. A country accustomed to strict population control, where it was extremely rare to read about shoot-outs in the streets, found itself with murder rates comparable to those of narcostates in Latin America during their worst periods. The years 1995 and 1996 were not much better as far as homicides went (respectively 30.6 and 26.5 per 100,000 inhabitants). Recorded crimes were higher in 1995 than in 1994.

The traditional *vory* suffered significant losses during the

Great Mob War. On the basis of the biographies of more than six thousand members that I have collected and systematized over the years, I have been able to reconstruct the deaths of the members of the brotherhood. As early as 1989, the *vory* – the bosses of the Russian mafia – began to die at a rapid rate; there were almost eighty-nine fatalities in 1991–2. The years 1993–4 were lethal for the brotherhood, which registered approximately 159 victims in total, and 1995–6 continued to be a period of considerable violence. There were sixty-two deaths in 1995, sixty-nine in 1996, fifty-one in 1997, and forty-four in 1998. In 1997–8 the *vory* were still being killed in large numbers – ninety-five in that year.

When it seemed that they would be swept away by the newcomers, many *vory* reorganized under the banner of a new group, which was to be the most powerful criminal organization born from the ashes of the Soviet Union: Solntsevskaya bratva, 'the Brotherhood of the Sun'. The organization, born in a modest working-class neighbourhood of Solntsevo (Solar) in the west-southwest area of Moscow, spread through a series of gyms run by a former waiter, bodybuilder, and card player. By the early 1980s he controlled various activities in the black market and had amassed a large fortune, which he laundered in Europe and the United States. By the end of that decade the Brotherhood of the Sun was in full expansion and had absorbed many of the traditional *vory*. In an FBI report from 1995, it was defined as the most important group in Eurasian organized crime in terms of wealth, influence, and economic control. In a 2014 *Fortune* magazine investigation into the world's top criminal organizations, the Brotherhood of the Sun ranked first, with annual earnings of $8.5 billion, which outranked the Camorra,

the 'Ndrangheta, and the Mexican Sinaloa Cartel. Some
estimates, perhaps overstated, suggest that the organization had between 5,000 and 9,000 members. It adheres to
the principles of the *vory* and has a flexible structure: it
consists of a series of autonomous brigades (*brigady*) that
operate under the collective name Brotherhood of the Sun
and is governed by a council of twelve people that meets
regularly in different parts of the world. The proceeds are
shared. 'All the criminal activities of the Solntsevskaya
[Brotherhood of the Sun] feed into a common fund that
is administered by several banks', a former member of
the organization told the FBI. Ivan'kov attached his group
to this new structure, ready to counter the dominance
of Chechens, Azerbaijanis, and others, but then suddenly
decided to leave for the United States.

Two versions are in circulation about the reasons for
Ivan'kov's departure. According to some, he was forced
to flee in order to avoid being killed by the Chechen fac-
tion of post-Soviet organized crime. According to others,
he was sent by the head of the Brotherhood of the Sun
to explore new opportunities overseas and forge alliances
with Russian mobsters in America. This second theory is
supported, for example, by a confidential report from the
Central Operational Service (SCO) of the Italian police,
which in the 1990s investigated the presence of Russian
mafia in Rome and its contacts with Italian banks (especially the Nuovo Banco Ambrosiano) in Moscow. Ivan'kov
himself claimed that he emigrated because he could not
live in 'a country where human, civil, and constitutional
rights are violated in a mean and vile way, where the scum
[police] are the real criminals'.

Ivan'kov arrived in New York from Budapest in March
1992. He was carrying a letter that invited him to take up

a job at a film production company, Studio 12°. His documents were in order, and no one stopped him. He went to live in Brighton Beach and shortly afterwards married a singer, in a fictitious marriage designed to give him a green card; his employment in the film industry was equally fictitious. Undoubtedly Ivan'kov maintained contact with the Brotherhood of the Sun while he stayed in America. For example, he was intercepted while speaking with other leaders of the organization, and in 1993 he attended a meeting in Miami along with several Russian mobsters. According to information gathered by the Italian SCO from American intelligence sources, the meeting discussed the expansion of the Brotherhood of the Sun in America and Italy.

In the United States Ivan'kov engaged in his favourite activity, 'solving problems', which meant recovering debts, retrieving stolen property, and more generally acting as the ultimate arbiter of informal or outright illegal deals. Russian entrepreneurs wanting to invest in the United States turned to the Little Japanese for advice and protection (neither of which was free). When the American police got hold of his agenda, they found many references to *zus*, a term in the language of thieves in law that refers to disputes over profits that must be resolved by a criminal authority. In other words, Ivan'kov was the one who decided the outcome of a dispute between more or less legitimate entrepreneurs. For example, in 1993 Alexander Volkov, president of the investment company Summit International, had borrowed $2.7 million from a Moscow bank. Having lost the money in very dubious investments, Volkov and his partner had no intention of returning anything. Creditors then turned to Ivan'kov, who decreed that Volkov had to repay $3.5 million – the initial amount plus interest. Broke, frightened of the reputation of the Little Japanese, and still reeling from the shock of his father's murder in Moscow, Volkov turned to the FBI for help. In June 1995, US authorities began tracking Ivan'kov down. Agent James Moody was tasked with finding him. Moody told Robert I. Friedman, journalist and author of *Red Mafia* (2000): 'At first, all we had was a name . . . We were looking around, looking around, looking around, and had to go out and really beat the bushes.' Then, when they located him, they were surprised by where he was. 'And then we found out that he was in a luxury condo in Trump Towers', in Manhattan.

There is a red thread connecting Donald Trump to the Soviet world. At crucial moments in the future US president's career, when western banks were hesitant to lend him money, funds from the Soviet Union seemed to provide him with vital support. The Trump Tower opened its doors in 1983, the first customers being Russians who paid in cash. Some had made their fortune in the black market, while others might have been undercover agents. To transfer money to the United States, they used banks in Israel, Luxembourg, and Switzerland. For example, in 1984, Trump sold five apartments to David Bogatin, a figure in Russian organized crime, for $6 million. Bogatin used the properties to carry out fraud, gasoline smuggling, and money laundering – as American investigators discovered. In 1987 he was sentenced to two years in prison for tax evasion. Bogatin confessed, but as soon as he was released on parole fled to Poland. After a few years he was extradited to the United States, where he completed his sentence.

In the early 1990s there was a second wave of emigrants to the United States from the former Soviet Union, some with access to funds from the Communist Party or the Soviet state. Others were members of organized crime, like Ivan'kov. When Moody and his agents were about to arrest him in the Trump Tower apartment in 1995, Ivan'kov had already disappeared. Moody persevered and, thanks to a tip, discovered that Ivan'kov was hiding at the Taj Mahal Casino in Atlantic City, 'one of the eight wonders of the world' – another property from Donald Trump's empire. The Taj Mahal was known for being the favourite hangout of Russian clients, who bet up to $5,000 at a time. A report on crime from the former Soviet Union that had taken root in the eastern United States confirmed that casinos like the Taj Mahal were used to launder Russian money. In its first year and a half of operation, the Taj Mahal was fined 106 times for violating money laundering laws. In 1998 the tax office, the infamous Internal Revenue Service, punished the Taj Mahal also for dozens of violations. When the agents arrived, Ivan'kov had disappeared again. In the end he was arrested in the Brighton Beach apartment of his American lover, with $75,000 in cash and a gun hidden in a sock, which he threw into a hedge under the window. The agents also recovered Ivan'kov's agenda, which contained phone and fax numbers for Trump Tower offices. To what extent can these events be linked to Trump himself? On the one hand, a real estate developer cannot be responsible for what his customers do. On the other hand, as the *Guardian* journalist Luke Harding argues in *Collusion*, 'Russian clients were a core part of Trump's business. This has been true since he started out as a builder.'

An interesting story connects Perm (the city of my fieldwork), Trump, and a villa in Florida: the businessman Dmitrii Rybolovlev acquired control of a potassium mine near Perm in the 1990s. In 2010 he sold his stake for

$5.3 billion, moved to Monaco, and became a major art collector (he was the one-time owner of the *Salvator mundi* attributed to Leonardo). In 2008 Rybolovlev bought from Donald Trump, for $95 million, a Florida villa that Trump had purchased four years earlier for $41.4 million; thus he earned the tycoon $53.6 million. This was an extraordinary profit. American investigators who looked into the ties between Trump and Putin found it strange that, although the American real estate market was collapsing, Trump managed to sell for such an astronomical figure a house that had been on the market for two years. Rybolovlev never set foot in the villa and soon had it demolished: allegedly he had not noticed that mould was everywhere. The oligarch's spokesperson maintained that the investment was legal, was not politically motivated, and turned out to be profitable.

Let us return to Ivan'kov. He was finally put on trial for extortion, but the American police had not obtained a wiretap warrant, which made the prosecution case rather weak. It was only thanks to phone intercepts conducted by Canadian authorities that the New York prosecutor managed to present irrefutable evidence of Ivan'kov's activities in the United States. After several weeks of hearings, Ivan'kov was convicted of extortion and of entering into a fictitious marriage and was sentenced, in January 1997, to nine years and seven months in prison. Ivan'kov said that, by comparison with the Soviet Gulag, the US Penitentiary Allenwood looked like a 'gilded cage' to him. There he did everything to build a reputation as a ruthless criminal. When a Latin American prisoner showed him the middle finger, he bit it with such force that the phalanx got severed. On the other hand, in an interview conducted from his prison for a Russian TV channel, Ivan'kov appears as a cultured person, speaking in elaborate sentences and using erudite quotations. In the interview, he claimed to be a victim of the Russian secret services for his fight against the Soviet regime.

Despite the convincing tone, it is hard to believe a single word he said. Incredibly, Ivan'kov did not serve the full sentence in this case either. In 2004 the Russian prosecutor requested his extradition for two murders committed in 1992, just before Ivan'kov left for the United States. The victims were two Turks. The extradition request was granted, and the Little Japanese was put on a plane to Moscow. However, the trial that ensued had many flaws, and Ivan'kov was acquitted. In July 2005 he was a free man again.

Ivan'kov resumed his activities as a peacemaker between criminal groups and law-skirting entrepreneurs. On 28 July 2009 something inconceivable happened. Ivan'kov and two bodyguards were having dinner at the Tay Elephant restaurant in Moscow, on the Khoroshevskoye highway. When they went out in the street, a sniper opened fire on Ivan'kov, who was seriously wounded in the stomach. The assailant was firing from a car parked on the opposite side. The rifle used was a Dragunov (SVD) with an optical sight. After taking the shots, the assassin disappeared into the night.

Ivan'kov was immediately taken to the hospital, where he underwent emergency surgery and was then put in a medically induced coma. Doctors did everything they could to save his life – unsuccessfully. He died on 9 October 2009. The stomach wound had caused peritonitis, bringing an end to the earthly life of a legendary figure in Russian crime. He was sixty-nine years old. For his send-off, his associates spared no expense: the oak coffin equipped with light and air conditioning is said to have cost US$100,000. Overall, the funeral bill was a million dollars. On the day of the wake, traffic around the Vagan'kovskoye cemetery came to a halt. About two hundred bosses of the Russian mafia attended, conveying their condolences with flower wreaths (some paid their respects only after dark, to avoid being spotted by the police). The Little Japanese was buried next to his mother, in a temporary wooden grave. The monument I saw during my trip in 2017 was erected a few years later.

For a long time, law enforcement could not identify Ivan'kov's murderers. It seemed that their names would remain unknown forever. But in February 2020 there was a breakthrough. The police arrested three people and charged two more in absentia. They all hailed from the Georgian breakaway region of Abkhazia. By 2023 they had all received long prison sentences, but two of them, Astamur Butba (who fired the fatal shot) and Nugzar Papava, managed to avoid serving them by hiding in Abkhazia, a country that does not have an extradition treaty with Russia. In September 2023 a journalist from *Izvestiya* tracked down the forty-six-year-old Papava in a village 20 km away from Sukhumi. He now leads a pastoral lifestyle, has pigs grazing in his yard, and grows figs, bananas, and peaches. The view of Abkhazia's mountains from his windows is breathtaking. Protesting his innocence, he says that he is willing to go to Russia but, alas, is under house arrest for the kidnapping of a businessman. Sadly, the long arm of the local law forces him to stay put and delays his return.

Who sent this team of five to kill the Little Japanese? The man behind the hit is Il'ya Simoniya (Makho), a thief in law who wanted to avenge the insult he suffered in the late 1980s, when Ivan'kov was transferred to the Tulun prison and refused to recognize his authority. Makho commanded the Irkutsk region at the time, but Ivan'kov managed to have his status revoked. To regain it, Makho had to kill Ivan'kov. And so he did, promising the assassins tens of millions of roubles. In the fall of 2019 Makho achieved his main goal: at a meeting of mafia bosses, he regained the title of thief in law, and now lives in Italy.

The story of Ivan'kov captures a crucial aspect of power in Russia. Mafia violence played a fundamental role in the criminal governance of the economy in the late Soviet period and even more so in the 1990s. When the black market exploded as a result of the prohibition of vodka, the cooperative movement, and large-scale privatization, the Soviet regime could not control the market. Unregulated capitalism generates a demand for order, for certainty. Legitimate state institutions were unable to limit the violence and to produce clear and fair rules. The likes of Ivan'kov stepped in.

CHAPTER 2

THE OLIGARCH
BORIS BEREZOVSKY

When the Great Mob War was raging on the streets of Moscow and the Russian economy was disintegrating, Yeltsin surrounded himself with a tight-knit cabal of loyalists, all living together in a group of presidential apartments on Rublyovo-Uspenskoye Street. This court of miracles included the president's daughter, a tennis coach, a journalist, a bodyguard, the prime minister, and the defence minister. Among them, fierce disputes erupted over who was entitled to greater privileges. The glue that bound Yeltsin's chosen elite was active engagement in plundering the state coffers and in selling everything possible to the highest bidder, while repression served to silence the opposition. Even the young reformist economists tasked with privatizing the economy were keenly interested in profiting from their roles. A straightforward mechanism for generating favours was to pay astronomical sums for an appearance at a conference or the rights to a book. The architect of the privatization programme that would ultimately transform the Russian economy in the 1992–3 period, Anatolii Chubais, received a $90,000 advance for a book. The bank that paid him the money was one of the main beneficiaries of his decisions. And it was also through a book that Boris Berezovsky, until then an entrepreneur and wheeler-dealer outside Yeltsin's power system, entered the president's inner circle.

In the winter of 1993–4, Yeltsin was looking for a publisher for his memoir, *The View from the Kremlin: The President's Journal.* The book recounted Yeltsin's first two years (1992–3) at the peak of the Russian political system. The ghostwriter was one Valentin Yumashev, a journalist who lacked particular narrative skills and had a rather shabby appearance. Yumashev had worked on Yeltsin's first book in 1989 and would later marry his daughter, in 2001. No one at the court understood why the president was so interested in maintaining a connection with this character. The answer became clear in time. Yumashev took on the task of finding a Russian publisher who would bear the publication costs of *The View from the Kremlin* and would eventually deposit the royalties into Yeltsin's London bank account. That elusive publisher turned out to be Boris Berezovsky, co-owner of a magazine where Yumashev acted as deputy editor. The entire operation was very dubious: several Russian publishers would have accepted the book, even paying the author an advance. Why involve an entrepreneur who was known at the time only for controlling the distribution of automobiles? In any case, Yeltsin expected to receive royalties of at least a million dollars. The book was printed in Finland, and Berezovsky – according to his account – spent $250,000. *The View from the Kremlin* was released in 1994 and was launched with great emphasis at the Presidential Club, a sports complex at 42 Kosygin Street that comprised tennis courts, a swimming pool, and a gym and had been founded by the president himself in 1993. The president spent a lot of time there, playing doubles with his tennis coach (later appointed minister of sport) at least twice a week.

Yeltsin showed gratitude to Berezovsky for his efforts and proposed him as a member of the club. From that moment on, Berezovsky became a figure of national importance. However, when Yeltsin realized that the royalties were rather thin, he became furious with both Yumashev and Berezovsky. The latter immediately took action, starting to deposit money at Barclays Bank in London. By the end of 1994 there were at least 3 million US dollars in the account, and Berezovsky publicly boasted of being Yeltsin's secret financier. Every month, Yumashev had brief meetings with the president, bringing him the interest, which amounted to about $16,000 in cash. At the end of each meeting, the president stored the money in the safe in his office.

Who was Boris Berezovsky? Born on January 23, 1946, he claimed to have lived 'a perfectly happy Soviet childhood'. His father, an engineer, had moved to Moscow from the Siberian city of Tomsk. After studying forestry, he specialized in applied mathematics and, in 1969, was hired at the prestigious Institute of Control Sciences, an institution where scientists of different backgrounds formed working groups to find efficient solutions to the management problems of the Soviet production system. Widespread antisemitism in the Soviet Union made it very difficult for individuals of Jewish origin such as Berezovsky to pursue a career in politics, economics, or academia. The institute at 65 Profsoyuznaya Street was one of the few oases of meritocracy. A researcher who attended the institute in the 1970s remembers it as 'a surprising place . . . in the quantity of unusual people – by their energy, their intellect, their originality. There was an extremely rich intellectual life . . . both scientific and humanitarian'.

Berezovsky possessed an analytical mind and the tenacity required for research. He authored three monographs and dozens of scientific essays and won several awards, including the Lenin Prize. For several years, he focused on solving a theorem central to his doctoral thesis but, by his own admission, he wasn't a brilliant scientist (the proof of that theorem turned out to be incorrect). He had instead an extraordinary amount of energy and knew how to navigate the system to obtain practical results such as research funds, equipment, and hands-on assistance for his colleagues. He could build relationships between people and institutions, plan conferences, host foreign scholars, and organize trips. At the same time he was a generator of ideas, leaving it to others to develop them. 'Half of the things he said didn't make sense, but the other half were genius', recalls a colleague. Within a few years, he became the director of the research group that specialized in decision theory, a branch of applied mathematics that had few practical applications during the Brezhnev stagnation in the 1970s and early 1980s. One of his responsibilities was to ensure that collaborators found housing, medicine, perhaps a car, and were thus free to dedicate themselves to research. Deep down, Berezovsky was a man of the world, not of science. If perestroika had not arrived, he would probably have become the rector of the institute.

His life changed thanks to an Italian car. The Soviet Zhiguli was produced in a colossal plant, Avtovaz, located in Tolyatti – a city on the Volga named after Palmiro Togliatti, leader of the Italian Communist Party. The plant, which faithfully reproduced Fiat's assembly line down to the smallest details, was built in 1967 by enthusiastic members of the Communist Youth League, the Komsomol. The industrial complex was immense; it had twenty-two entrances and the perimeter measured fourteen kilometres. Near the factory a city was built where workers and their families could live. The project was the brainchild of the party secretary, Leonid Brezhnev, who wanted to show the world that the Soviet Union could produce consumer goods just like the West and meet domestic demand. The first car to roll off the assembly line was a modified version of the Fiat 124, with a 1.2-liter engine. Three years later, the millionth Zhiguli was produced. Avtovaz came to contribute about 1 per cent of the country's gross domestic product. There was a non-obvious relationship between the institute and the factory. The research conducted by Berezovsky's centre had to have a practical application, in the hope that it would make the planned economy or the country's military machine more efficient. So Berezovsky, who dreamed of owning a Zhiguli himself, developed a project to improve the production system of the Tolyatti automotive plant. The factory certified that the research had a positive impact on production, and the state reimbursed Berezovsky's institute.

Meanwhile history was unfolding, and Berezovsky realized that nothing would be the same again. In 1989 Soviet troops withdrew from Afghanistan, the Berlin Wall fell, and the deputies of the People's Congress were elected democratically. The planned economy could not be saved, and Berezovsky did not want to miss the opportunity to be part of the future. He decided to use his contacts at Avtovaz to get introduced to the company's chief, Vladimir Kadannikov, a manager of the new generation who was aware that the plant had to adapt to a new economic reality and who did not have too many scruples.

Berezovsky's offer was simple: to create a company that would manage relations with Italian colleagues. At first, Kadannikov did not understand what the benefits could be: why create an intermediary to do what Avtovaz was already doing? But he soon appreciated the potential of the project and became a partner in Logovaz, the new company created by Berezovsky. This entity became a tool for defrauding Avtovaz. Cars were produced by the state at artificially low prices. Instead of being distributed to those in need, according to the dictates of the plan, they were sold to intermediaries such as Logovaz, which in turn sold them at market prices and in foreign currency. Without paying anything when receiving the cars, the intermediaries returned the proceeds to the company months later and in roubles, at a time when inflation was 2,000 per cent per year. The state was being robbed, and figures such as Berezovsky became millionaires. Managers received hefty bribes, while workers were paid very late. The intermediaries were protected by criminal groups stationed in the plants to take their agreed-upon share of cars. Real battles erupted in Tolyatti in the early 1990s. For about a decade starting in 1992, the war for control over Avtovaz cost as many as nine hundred lives. Valerii Ivanov, founder and director of a local newspaper and author of many investigations into crimes connected to the plant, faced numerous threats and non-lethal attacks from the start. In 2002 he was assassinated while getting out of his car to enter the building in which he lived with his family. His successor, Aleksei Sidorov, met the same fate after six months, in 2003 (the newspaper closed down in 2014; the two murders have never been solved). From the second half of the 1990s until 2002, at least three other journalists were slain, and a fourth died in very suspicious circumstances. It's incredible

that Berezovsky, protected by a gang of Chechen mobsters, managed to become a millionaire while around him
hundreds of people were killed every year.

I was in Moscow when the war was raging in Tolyatti.
There I was often a guest in my uncle's house, the cor-
respondent for the Italian newspaper *Sole 24 ore*. He had
met my aunt when they were both students in Moscow, in
the late 1960s, and went to work at the NATO headquarters before joining the Italian counterpart of the *Financial
Times*. In addition to his journalistic duties, he was a kind
of informal ambassador for Italian businesses in Russia and
an authority on the country. He knew everybody in town.
Thanks to his good offices, I was admitted into the presence of Berezovsky, who had interests in Italy through
Avtovaz. I believe that my affiliation with a prominent
Anglo-Saxon university sparked a certain curiosity in the
former academic. Also, he could not say no to my uncle.

Several exclusive clubs for the new rich had opened in
Moscow at the time. State officials, entrepreneurs, and
gangsters met behind closed doors to discuss business,
to place large bets on the table, and to be entertained by
young and attractive women on the lookout for fortune
in the capital. Although they epitomized the new capitalist
Russia, the clubs reproduced the system of restricted access
to privileges and fun that characterized the Soviet nomen-
klatura (as a source told me). One of the most famous
clubs was the Grand Dynamo, where ecstasy was said to
be consumed and the night was filled with wild dancing.
Berezovsky, who didn't want to be outdone, restored a
late nineteenth-century mansion in the centre of Moscow,
once owned by a Russian merchant, for almost $2 million
and established there his own club – Club Logovaz, furnished in Empire style. To enter, you had to pass several

security checks, but then you found yourself in an oasis of opulence, where dozens of scantily clad young girls strolled nonchalantly. Berezovsky wanted to make people believe that the most important decisions of the Russian government were made at the tables of his club.

I met him for only a few minutes. He spoke quickly, and the cell phone rang continuously. When I told him that I was a student at a prestigious university, he replied that producing science was a real talent and that he wanted to help young talented people. He asked me to explore the possibility of establishing scholarships in his name, an idea I dropped as soon as I stepped outside. Nevertheless, I had time to ask him a couple of questions about Russian capitalism. He replied: 'I was the first to create a market economy in this country, but here nothing is done without an understanding with the right people.' He seemed convinced that he had played a fundamental role in the country's progress, rather than being part of the legalized theft of the 1990s. I did not contradict him, but I noticed that the word he used to refer to the 'understanding' between the right people was *ponyatiye* – a word taken from the jargon of thieves in law. I found that linguistic choice illuminating. When he suggested that perhaps we could meet in London one day, I understood that my time was up. An assistant ushered us into a small room, where some Italian entrepreneurs were chatting amicably. Shortly after our meeting, Berezovsky fell victim to a serious attempt on his life. An Opel filled with explosives was detonated as his armoured Mercedes passed by. The driver died instantly, decapitated in the explosion, while Berezovsky emerged practically unscathed. The wars of Tolyatti had reached the rarefied atmosphere of Moscow clubs. No one could feel safe.

Berezovsky's dream in the early 1990s was not to end up as an intermediary between managers of state enterprises and consumers. He wanted to be the boss. He shared this aspiration with the president. While the West believed that Yeltsin was committed to creating a modern market economy, he aimed to rebuild an autocratic society, with himself and his court in control of the country's resources – a version of the Soviet model, but without any socialist aspirations. However, to achieve this goal, the president had to get rid of the forces that were hostile to him. The institution that stood most in the way of his plans was the parliament. Elected in 1990, it was composed of Gorbachev-type reformers, old-school communists, and liberals. It had opposed the price liberalization of 1991, which had destroyed the savings of the Russians, and now it stood against the privatization plan that Anatolii Chubais, the president's technocratic ally, had started to implement in October 1992. Privatization was proceeding swiftly. In December 1992 only eighteen companies had been sold, but by April 1993 as many as 582 were in private hands and that figure rose to 2,418 by the end of June. The battle over properties became a battle over democracy.

In March 1993, the parliament was preparing a motion to impeach the president. On 20 March Yeltsin declared emergency rule: he would impose martial law if the political crisis was not resolved. Two days later, on 22 March, Yeltsin drew up a secret plan for a coup to be carried out in case the parliament charged him. A presidential decree to dissolve parliament was ready. Special units equipped with gas to be released in the Chamber were on high alert. But on 28 March the deputies opposed to Yeltsin failed to gain a majority and the proposal for impeachment was rejected. The planned coup was put back in the drawer, for now.

The conflict between the president and the parliament continued throughout the summer, with mutual accusations, until the president ordered the dissolution of the assembly on 21 September. The Supreme Court pointed out that the president's decision was unconstitutional. About a hundred people barricaded themselves inside the building known as the Russian White House and were ready to resist. If they did not come out by 4 October, the special forces of the Ministry of Internal Affairs would storm the palace, Yeltsin thundered. On 3 October at least 10,000 defenders of parliamentary democracy headed towards the White House and the Russian TV headquarters. A group managed to break through the police cordon and enter the seat of parliamentary democracy. A second crowd headed for the TV headquarters but failed to storm the building: elite units barricaded in the television studios opened fire, causing dozens of deaths. The station was not taken. On 4 October, Yeltsin ordered tanks to enter the centre of Moscow. They positioned themselves on the Novy Arbat Bridge and began shelling the parliament building. A fire broke out on the upper floors, and documents flew in the Moscow sky. Just two years after the attempted coup against Gorbachev, violence returned to the centre of the capital, this time at the hands of the leader the West had hailed as a defender of democracy. While tanks were firing, special forces units occupied the building. By the evening, the parliamentarians surrendered. The number of victims of the events on 3 and 4 October varies between 142 (the official estimate) and as many as five hundred dead and wounded.

On 5 October, in a phone call from Air Force One, President Clinton expressed approval to the Russian president: 'Dear Boris, you did everything you had to do, and

I congratulate you on how you handled the matter.' The United States endorsed a very serious crime. Two months after the attack on the Russian parliament, Yeltsin called a referendum to adopt a new constitution. According to the proposal, the president concentrated immense power on himself, effectively sidelining parliament. The proposal was approved by 60 per cent of voters, with a turnout of 53 per cent. Scholars have questioned the electoral results, claiming widespread fraud and irregularities. The year 1993 marks the beginning of the end of the very brief democratic spell in Russia. When, in June 1996, Yeltsin was re-elected to the presidency with crucial help from Berezovsky, he ordered his collaborators to develop a 'national ideology', in defiance of the still secular nature of the post-Soviet constitution. In a speech to the Federation Council, he declared that, without a new state ideology, the very existence of the nation was in danger. Vladimir Putin just picked up an already existing project, which he now continues.

Once parliament was subdued, privatization could be completed. Instead of privatizing gradually, starting with small businesses, the president's men sold off the entire industrial system in a few years. Yuri Luzhkov, the mayor of Moscow, likened this process to 'a drunkard in the street selling off his belongings for a pittance'. Russians couldn't benefit from it. The voucher that each citizen received to buy shares in state-owned companies put on the market was worth the equivalent of two bottles of vodka. Those who had the money to hoard assets were figures like Berezovsky, who had accumulated millions in the early 1990s and had the Kremlin's support. The value of the companies was so low that, once you purchased them, it was more advantageous to strip them of everything valuable and resell the land. There was no incentive to invest in reviving production and defending employment. Not surprisingly, industrial production reached a record low. And yet there was a method to this madness; it made a few people very rich. The madness unleashed violent wars for control over strategic sectors such as gas, oil, precious metals, aluminium, and television.

One of the main beneficiaries of privatization was Boris Berezovsky, who fulfilled his dream of becoming the boss of important sectors of the Soviet industry. In a few years he came to control state television, the oil company Sibneft, the third largest in the country, and the airline Aeroflot. He was also responsible for a colossal fraud against Russians: in 1993–4, he launched the sale of 'vouchers' for the construction of a new plant, designed to operate alongside Avtovaz. Russians bought certificates worth about $50 million, but the project did not materialize and no one was compensated. Meanwhile Berezovsky used part of the money to acquire 34 per cent of Avtovaz. He was never prosecuted for this fraud and continued to enjoy Kremlin's support.

In 1996 Berezovsky threw himself headlong to ensure Yeltsin's re-election.

At first, everybody thought that Yeltsin would lose. Thus the head of the presidential guards concocted a plan to postpone the vote by two years and declare a state of emergency. But there was no need: the West came to the rescue once again. In 1996, the United States teamed up with Berezovsky and other oligarchs to influence the vote directly: secret loans, International Money Fund assistance with no questions asked, electoral strategists, and a visit by Clinton during the campaign were all deployed. TV stations such as ORT (owned by Berezovsky) and NTV (owned by another oligarch) were enlisted in the effort. The principles of independent journalism were compromised. Vladimir

Pozner, a leading TV journalist, said that in 1996 'the age of innocence passed. . . everything that happened since had its roots there'.

Fast forward to 2000, and you'll find Berezovsky at the centre of the plots that brought Putin to the presidency – a story perhaps too long to recount. Suffice it to say that his fortune took a turn for the worse when Putin, whom he believed to be his protégé, decided to free himself from the influence of the oligarchs once he had been elected president in 2000. Berezovsky had not understood that the violent transition to the market would devour its children. Sheltered in England to avoid imprisonment, Berezovsky became a pathetic figure on the London scene, desperately searching for a way to regain the spotlight. In August 2012 he lost a major legal action against Roman Abramovich, his former partner in the oil company Sibneft. He had become one of the most bitter critics of the regime, but lacked credibility.

He even tried to get back in touch with me; I had become a professor of criminology at Oxford by then. I declined his invitation. When I learned of his death in 2013, I wondered whether it was suicide. I arranged a confidential meeting with the Oxford police inspector in charge of the investigation, who agreed to tell a selected group of fellows about the inquiry in a private room at my college. It was an event that I remember with affection and nostalgia. I had invited my friend John le Carré and his wife Jane. The writer had the opportunity to express his opinions on the role of intelligence services in the contemporary world, views that shall remain confidential but, alas, were not flattering. After dinner, the officer reassured us that the cause of Berezovsky's death was suicide. They found no traces of suspicious substances, and the bathroom door, where he hanged himself, was closed from the inside. At that juncture in his life, Berezovsky teetered on the brink of bankruptcy, residing as a guest in his former wife's home. He felt utterly defeated. A journalist who interviewed him a few days before his demise reported that Berezovsky seemed to be in a state of deep confusion. Therefore he might have committed suicide, but some aspects of his death remained unclear. The English magistrate refused to rule out murder entirely.

Boris Berezovsky was the most ambitious of the oligarchs of the 1990s but was by no means the architect of the market economy, contrary to what he told me in his Moscow club. Rather, this man was one of the major contributors to the failures of post-Soviet Russia in that crucial decade, when neither a free market nor a democracy saw the light of day. But he was not the main culprit. To promote the kind of privatization that would eventually benefit the likes of Berezovsky, Yeltsin used the army to crash the parliament in 1993. That event was the key turning point, marking the beginning of the end of democracy. The 1994 constitution was instrumental in making the regime authoritarian and ushering in the creation of the so-called system of the power vertical, to be fully exploited by Putin later. Privatization was part of a violent political transition towards an authoritarian regime, benefiting as it did a small circle and ultimately leading to Putin's presidency.

CHAPTER 3

THE CONVICT
SERGEI SAVEL'EV

'Peace to our Common Home. Prosperity to the community of thieves in law.' Thus begins one of the most significant and controversial documents ever produced by the Russian mafia. Appearing in the major prisons of the Federation in early December 2021, it is handwritten in beautiful script, with some words underlined repeatedly. The first text to be signed by the 'totality of thieves in law' (the community of bosses, who also included Ivan'kov), it proposes a radical reinterpretation of the principles that govern daily life in Russian prisons. The document is a response to dozens of videos that emerged in November 2021 showing how authorities in many penitentiaries rape prisoners unwilling to cooperate. The videos were smuggled out by a former inmate now hiding in France, a reverse Edward Snowden. Putin's harsh treatment of non-aligned inmates and dissidents is changing the rules of the criminal world: today it is the mafia that invokes 'humanity and understanding' for the victims of torture and denounces the regime.

To understand the historical significance of the December document, we must enter a Russian prison – an experience one would not wish upon one's worst enemy. A typical cell should accommodate no more than a dozen people. As a rule, you will find about thirty. In addition to being overwhelmed by the smell of bodies squeezed one on top of another and by acrid human sweat, you can see the latrine and a small table. Not everyone has a plank bed: to lie down, you have to work shifts, even three a night. The indistinct noise of voices stops and everyone looks at the newcomer, who would probably notice a couple of inmates crouched near the toilet. They are not just any prisoners: these poor sods belong to the caste of the untouchables. The initial moments pose the most significant challenges for a newcomer. Everyone expects him to make a mistake: that he speaks to the untouchables, maybe even that he goes to lie in the same bunk. One misstep is paid for with degradation to the lowest caste in the prison hierarchy.

The epithets for the untouchables in Russian criminal jargon are innumerable: 'offended', 'anointed', 'marginalized', 'cockerels', 'mice', 'comb', 'daisies', 'blue'. According to the unwritten but strict rules of prisons, homosexuals, those who have touched a penis, those who have been sprinkled with urine by other inmates, and those who have committed acts of paedophilia fall automatically into the category of the damned. Even if one is guilty of no more than disobeying the rules or coming into conflict with cell bosses – say, for not paying a gambling debt, or for being a spy – one can be demoted to the caste of the untouchables. At that point, life becomes a nightmare. 'It's worse than a death sentence', a former inmate once told me. Untouchables eat alone, wash in a separate sink, and spend their detention years cleaning out latrines and sewers. The other inmates cannot take anything from their hands or speak to them. Their food is placed in a separate fridge and their cutlery is marked with a hole. Everything they touch becomes impure. They suffer harassment of all kinds, including sexual, from authoritative prisoners such as thieves in law and their allies. Prison culture is homophobic and condemns passive homosexuality, but active homosexuality is widespread and tolerated. The untouchables are often very young and inexperienced boys who soon fall ill with AIDS (interestingly, in women's prisons homosexuals are instead at the top of the criminal hierarchy). Those who consort with the untouchables or show human compassion towards them risk being assimilated to them. A common saying in Russian prisons is 'only the life of the cockerel is worse than Kolyma'. Known as the white crematorium, Kolyma was the toughest camp region in the Soviet system.

The newcomer must protect himself not only from the thieves in law but also from the administration, which often manipulates informal rules so as to subjugate and harass the prison population. One of the simplest ways to make life impossible for a dissident or notorious criminal is to convict him of paedophilia. That way he will immediately enter the caste of the untouchables, even if the accusation is completely unfounded (it must be said that the criminal world does not always believe official charges and suspends judgement until it has collected independent evidence through a parallel investigation). Another strategy, adopted in certain prisons, is to use the untouchables to rape newcomers. The latter usually spend a fortnight in quarantine before being taken to the cell. During this period prison officials try to understand whether the recruit will be willing to admit his guilt (real or presumed) at trial and to cooperate by being an informant and denouncing others if necessary, or will be a hothead, determined to assert his rights and to rebel against abuses. Those who resist will be covered in urine, raped, and beaten to death.

Vladimir Pereverzin, a manager of the Yukos Company who spent seven years in jail, said he was faced with the following choice: either you sign your confession or you become an untouchable. Ivan Astashin was imprisoned for nearly ten years, between the ages of eighteen and twenty-eight, first in Krasnoyarsk and then in Norilsk, for throwing a Molotov bomb at a Federal Security Service (FSB) office (the damage was limited to broken glass). Ivan speaks to me from the kitchen of his small Moscow apartment; he has a penetrating gaze and a bald head. 'The system of untouchables would not exist if the prison administration were not complicit. It provides separate tables, fridges, special shower times and so on. These people are useful because they do jobs that nobody wants to do. In my unit, there were about 150 inmates and fifteen untouchables. When the number dropped, the administration found others.' Ivan, who works now for an association that defends prisoners' rights, confirms to me that today about 15 per cent of the entire male prison population in Russia is in the caste of the untouchables: more than 60,000 people, a number that, if confirmed, horrifies. That torture was widespread has been known for years, but until now there was a lack of irrefutable evidence apart from victim testimonies. A lawyer representing the untouchables, Aleksandr Vinogradov, said that, from 2013 to 2020, these inmates filed 4,300 petitions to the European Court of Human Rights – without any result. The court sent the complaint back to the Russian ministry, which wrote to the prison, which, after a thorough investigation, concluded that the petition was unfounded.

Things changed all of a sudden thanks to a thirty-one-year-old young Belarusian, Sergei Savel'ev.

Sergei answers my questions from a safe location in France, where he applied for asylum. He arrived there on the night of 15 October 2021, after a daring to escape from Russia at the end of seven years spent in prison. During the last two years of detention, he collected more than a thousand videos of torture carried out by prison officials. The footage has started to appear and has already triggered an earthquake, which is felt in cells across the post-Soviet world and in the secret rooms of the Kremlin.

Sergei does not fit the image of a professional criminal; he looks rather like the computer technician you call if you have connection problems. He is small and wears glasses. During our conversation, he switches from polished and grammatically sophisticated Russian to prison slang. 'Yes, it's me, the one who passed those terrible images to the non-governmental association Gulagu.net.' His voice betrays the difficulty of talking about the inferno he lived. The conversation struggles a bit to get going, but then it flows.

In 2013 Sergei was arrested in Krasnodar for drug offences: he agreed to deliver a package that soon turned out to contain prohibited substances, and he was arrested immediately. In retrospect, this looks like an entrapment operation designed to make some local policemen look good. 'It's a simple and sad story, like many others.' He spent more than a year and a half in a prison near Krasnodar, awaiting trial. 'The cell was disgusting, the plaster fell on your head, you took turns to sleep, and the cockroaches were monstrous creatures, huge, with long red hairs, which rose from the sewers.'

When he was finally sentenced, he was sent to Saratov, a prison that had a bad reputation. 'The Saratov authorities think that the Krasnodar penitentiary is "black", that is, controlled by thieves in law, and therefore they want to make you "change colour", by hook or by crook.' This treatment takes place in the quarantine cells, where the new arrivals spend two weeks. There the *aktivisti* operate: these are prisoners recruited as informers and appointed to various official positions, such as head prefect of a detachment dormitory. The *aktivisti* constitute a parallel informal hierarchy. 'They ask you questions, try to figure out whether you will be a troublemaker, and beat you savagely', says Sergei.

Once he arrived in the correctional colony, Sergei was assigned to the infirmary, where he was tasked with some office duties. He filled out forms, took minutes, sorted out calls, entered data into a computer. He would spend the whole day in the office and return to his cell only late in the evening. In 2016 he fell ill with pneumonia, and the doctor on duty suspected that he also had tuberculosis. To do the X-rays, he was transferred to the Regional Tuberculosis Hospital Number 1, universally known by the acronym OTB-1, which was famous not so much for its diagnostic and therapeutic excellence as for being a torture centre. Sergei desperately tried not to go, but to no avail. After a series of tests, he discovered that he never had tuberculosis. But he was there now and could no longer return to his previous post. The *aktivisti* kept him under observation for a while, and then decreed that he was a reliable person and could be useful in the OTB-1. Thus he ended up working in the hospital command office. It was a job that he did not mind, similar to the previous one in that it allowed him to spend as little time as possible in the cell. In addition to various administrative tasks, making photocopies and sorting the archive, he also had to download the footage recorded by the body cameras worn by agents. 'It took some computer skills to perform this task', he tells me.

In the beginning he saw nothing of interest: a policeman inspecting the canteen, another entering and leaving a dormitory, a third one visiting a warehouse. All this time he knew that he was under close observation. 'After about two years, the turning point arrived: they trusted me enough, to the point of giving me the torture videos, with the task of deleting them or forwarding them to other offices.' The tortures do not happen by chance; they are planned down to the smallest detail, in rooms without fixed cameras on the wall, says Sergei. A perpetrator brings a portable video camera, simple but effective, and films the entire event. 'Everyone knew that these things were happening, but until I saw them with my own eyes they didn't seem real. I started watching the footage and was disgusted. At first I didn't know what to do. Then I decided to copy them.'

The plan took shape around 2019, when Sergei decided to duplicate and hide the files they delivered to him. Sometimes he had to cut the copying of files short, at other times he was under strict surveillance and unable to act. In the end, the quantity of the stolen material is extraordinary: two terabytes of data, thousands of videos collected in less than two years. Sergei ran a huge risk. The images are irrefutable. 'Where did you find the strength?' I ask him. 'I do not know. I just did it. The most important thing for me was to come up with a plan. To do this, I had to encrypt the files securely. I was having a hard time staying calm, the stress was enormous, but in the end I made it.' Once Sergei's office was searched by officials from Moscow: they came looking for compromising material for an investigation that did not concern him. The files he had hidden were not found.

When his sentence ended, he returned to live in Belarus and, starting in February 2021, began to send documents to the Biarritz-based NGO Gulagu.net, started and headed by the human rights activist Vladimir Osechkin. 'At first we could not believe that the material was authentic, we suspected it was a provocation by the FSB to get us in trouble. Then we began to think it was genuine and came from a prison guard. Only on 24 September did Sergei reveal his identity; he told us that he was in danger and that he wanted to escape from Russia. Even then, we weren't 100 percent sure. But soon we started to trust him, after gathering information from other inmates who knew him. Sergei did it all by himself, he is a hero of our time', Osechkin tells me from the Gulagu.net office in Biarritz. When Sergei realized that his identity had been compromised, he fled to France via Turkey and Tunisia and asked for political asylum.

Some have cast doubt on this version of events, speculating that Sergei was probably allowed to smuggle the videos to embarrass the head of the prison administration. 'I think this was a special operation by the FSB aimed at removing [general Aleksandr] Kalashnikov', commented Olga Romanova – a well-known financial journalist who founded the association Russia behind Bars in 2008, after her husband's arrest – in an interview in *Current Time*. On 11 September 2023, the opposition magazine *Proekt* published a critical article of Vladimir Osechkin.

In any case, there is no doubt that the videos were genuine. The films began airing on 10 November, 2021, on the Gulagu.net YouTube channel. They are too disturbing to watch in full: the victims are held still while they are raped, the screams break our eardrums, resistance is futile. In an episode of 25 June 2020, a man orders a prisoner, who has his hands tied to the bed and his legs raised on the headboard, to utter his name loud and clear. The operator frames the face in the foreground, together with the ropes that tie the inmate, while another man holds him by the legs. The victim is then recorded from the side, while somebody rapes him, without a condom. Even those who joined the brotherhood of thieves in law were targeted. In footage recorded on 10 April 2020, a young man is seen naked, lying on his stomach, with his hands tied with duct tape behind his back. The torturer plants a military boot on his shoulder blades, calls him by name, and asks: 'Who are you in life?' The prisoner replies: 'Nobody, I'm a beggar.' A voiceover adds: 'You are a cockerel.' The other continues to press the boot on the prisoner's head and apostrophes him: 'This is the kind of thief in law you want to be. . .' Torture has just started but the young *vor* has already disavowed the brotherhood. If released, the video will mean automatic expulsion. Apart from members of the fraternity, others who are targeted include those who protest, those who write complaints against the administration, those who do not want to withdraw a testimony, those who have escaped from the camp, or those who do not want to carry out certain onerous tasks. Victims are also asked to change lawyers, if these are too diligent in their work. If you refuse, you know what awaits you. I was struck by the realization that the Orthodox Church Chapel is a mere 100 meters from this horrific place, yet Christian charity couldn't be further away.

The *aktivisti* are prisoners themselves. 'How is it possible that convicts commit such despicable crimes?' I ask Sergei, with a dose of naivety. 'Many of them were also raped. In prison, there are no people whose fate has not been distorted, whose psyche has not been damaged. I can understand why the guards and their allies inflict such pain, but I cannot justify them. Most of them are not sadists, they do it to survive; it is the system that generates monsters.' I ask him if he thinks his gesture could change anything. 'There is a risk that the perpetrators or low-ranking officials who appear in the videos will now be punished, and not those who ordered the rapes, who allowed them to take place. I hope my gesture pushes everyone to tell their story.' However, the informal code of the prison states that those who reveal having been raped join the ranks of the untouchables automatically, which makes it unlikely that prisoners in jail would confess. At least not until the code itself changes.

The December statement is a direct response to the release of Sergei's videos about a month earlier. The bosses decided to change the rules. Anyone who has been raped with a broom or a truncheon by the police (described as 'garbage' throughout the text) must not be turned into an untouchable. Those who have been violated with a penis cannot – rightfully – eat and drink together with the bosses, but – and here is the news – they must not be considered a 'cock' and can interact with other inmates. 'Humiliating and mocking' the victims of rapes perpetrated by the authorities and their thugs does not accord with manly behaviour. The thieves in law add: 'At a human level, one can only sympathize with them [the victims of rape].' The text continues with an appeal to those who have signed documents of collaboration with the authorities and are therefore afraid of becoming untouchable: 'It will not happen, it is not like that, a thousand times no. Be open about your situation and the men will help you' (by 'men' the authors refer to prisoners who respect the prison code). Those who have been attacked in Saratov or Irkutsk (another notorious torture centre) need not be afraid to tell their story. If a person is sincere, he will be treated with compassion. The text ends with a signature from 'the mass of thieves in law' and with an exhortation to the others to disseminate its content. According to Baza, the site that distributed the text, the statement was written during a conclave of thieves in law that was attended by Shakro the Younger (Zakhárii Kalashóv), a particularly influential boss.

As soon as the document was distributed on the Telegram channel of the Baza news agency, a debate ensued: is it authentic or is it a plant by the secret services? Conspiracy theories abound in a country like Russia. There are even people who claim that the document is a fake produced by the NGO Gulagu.net itself. A long article published in *Novaya Gazeta* on 15 December explored the issue by interviewing several experts and former prisoners. The general (but not unanimous) view is that the document is authentic. The analyses published on the MediaZona website come to the same conclusion. Eva Merkacheva, a journalist and human rights activist recently fired from the advisory commission of the Federal Prison Administration, said that she received the text from an inmate who is close to the world of thieves in law. 'I do not doubt its authenticity', she said. Sergei also tells me he does not believe it is a fake: 'My lawyers, collaborators, and former prison mates have all confirmed to me that it is authentic. Moreover, if this were not the case, a denial would have been published.'

In many ways, the December statement is similar to others that have been released by bosses over the past few years. For example positive concepts and keywords, such as mutual respect and unity, are underlined twice, with a firm hand. In documents written by the *vory*, names that are underlined twice indicate a person 'confident of his worth, who stands firmly on his own legs'. On the contrary, negative concepts, such as 'garbage' (the police) and disorder, have a double wavy underline, which symbolizes the 'vacillating and spineless' – 'those for whom thieves in law have no respect'. This practice is also used in statements of the same kind that I have examined in the past.

For example the Dubai Declaration – a text announcing the awarding of the title of boss to sixteen people during a ceremony in Dubai in 2012 (I discuss it in *Mafia Life*) – is structurally identical; and it is also handwritten and in italics. Again, the text begins by paying homage to the community of thieves in law, then proceeds to announce the names of the new bosses and the latest news. That document appeared on the PrimeCrime.ru site. Internet and Telegram channels are today the new prison radio, reaching everyone. Ivan Astashin from Moscow tells me, however, that in his penitentiary the declarations arrived on handwritten pieces of paper, brought by prisoners in transit. 'In my time there were often edicts on drug use. One, for example, ordered not to make excessive use of heroin and methadone (moderate use was ok!). Another strictly prohibited the use of new synthetic drugs, such as spice [a potent mix of herbs and chemicals]. Everyone, even us political prisoners, obeyed these orders.'

There is, however, a crucial difference between these statements and those of the past (called, in the criminal jargon, *progon*, in the singular). Previously such declarations bore the names of the bosses at the bottom, while the December one is not signed. Already in November, the influential thief in law Beso Kvinikhidze (Beso Rustavskii) spoke out in public against the practice of the *aktivisti* to violate prisoners: 'There are people who kill themselves in order not to lose their honour. And many are simply murdered by *aktivisti* during torture.' So why not sign? Ivan Astashin has no doubts as to why. He tells me: 'As a result of a provision in the Criminal Code introduced in 2019, whoever declares himself to be a thief in law risks a sentence of between eight and fifteen years; therefore nobody wants to sign with their own name.'

To ascertain the authenticity of the document myself, I contacted a high-ranking thief in law who lives in Greece today. In the past he helped me to decipher this world; he even gave me a gift – a pendant that represents a hand, which holds two dice in the palm while on its back is represented the eight-pointed star of the *vory-v-zakone* – the thieves in law. The pendant was produced in the laboratories of Greek prisons.

'Yes', he replied to me. 'We received the declaration in early December, when it had just come out. It is authentic and we know who wrote it.' He was keen to add that, even in the past, if a 'man' was raped with an object such as a stick or a broom or was doused with urine by guards or turncoat prisoners, he would not have joined the caste of the untouchables. 'It's another thing to be touched by a *** [penis]': in that case, the rule was – and continues to be – that the victim had to join the caste of the untouchables. The novelty is that the prisoner must now be treated with respect and compassion. My source adds a crucial detail: 'In our world, the document has created a lot of discussion. There is a profound division between those who accept the new resolution and those who defend the old rules. This debate can lead to conflict, and someone can get hurt.' Could this internal struggle resemble the one among the thieves in law that was unleashed during the Second World War, when some traditionalist bosses, opposed to any collaboration with the Soviet Union, refused to go and fight for it? 'Yes, it's possible', my informant replied, with the brevity that befits his character; but he added that he hoped that the conflict won't be as intense.

Nevertheless, the brotherhood is going through difficult times. There is no single boss of the bosses, no one who can speak for the entire Russian mafia. Many are in jail throughout Europe, and they have a different worldview from that of their counterparts in Russia. A conflict over the December declaration risks weakening the *vory* still further. Olga Romanova, the founder of the association Russia behind Bars, answers my questions from Berlin, where she recently took refuge: 'Thieves in law are under huge pressure from Putin's "vertical" power system', she tells me. Until about 2014–15 there was a *de facto* alliance between power and criminal structures. Then Putin realized that the thieves in law were getting too many advantages and he began to take a series of legislative measures against the brotherhood, to force them to cooperate from a position of inferiority.' In her opinion, this is also the period during which torture became widespread in prisons. From 2020, those who promote the culture of the 'criminal world' (loosely defined) are equated to extremists and terrorists. This is why Russian newspapers did not publish the December document in its entirety. As mentioned above, being a member of the brotherhood is now enough to put you in jail – a provision that echoes the 'mafia-type criminal association' to be found in other criminal codes. Defenders of the president point out that such provisions are borrowed from other countries, such as Italy and Georgia. Yet this is disingenuous. They are just part of a project designed to curtail freedom of the press and research. For instance, a new law on 'foreign agents' forces many newspapers and websites to prefix each of their articles with a text in all caps, stating: 'This content is produced by a foreign entity.' The NGO Memorial, founded by the Nobel laureate Andrei Sakharov in 1989 with the aim of keeping alive the memory and the study of Stalin's repressions, was dissolved in December 2021 precisely for having violated, according to the prosecution, the law on foreign agents.

Sergei's revelations are starting to have an effect. Once the initial videos went public, 400 inmates in Saratov reported sexual abuse, torture, and extortion. Similar footage emerged from four other prisons. Sergei tells me: 'There is a very high number of people who are not afraid to speak up. Nothing like this has ever been seen in the past.' The story of another Saratov inmate, Aleksei Makarov, confirms Sergei's data. According to Makarov, at least 100 people were abused and raped while he was there, between 2018 and 2020. Evidence of systematic torture also appeared in other prisons, such as Krasnoyarsk, Irkutsk, Angarsk, and Blagoveshchensk. In a video published by Gulagu.net, Denis Golikov admitted that he was a torturer in the Irkutsk camp. 'When I got to prison, I weighed 56 kilos and was 173 centimetres tall. The *aktivisti* stuffed me with steroids, and I ballooned to 117 kilos.' In order not to be raped himself, he became a perpetrator. According to Gulagu.net, mass abuses took place in Irkutsk in prison cells, to punish inmates who staged a protest. Between April and November of 2020, 400 inmates were raped, Golikov said.

The scandal prompted Putin to sack the director of the prison administration, Alexander Kalashnikov, the FSB general mentioned earlier. He replaced him with a deputy minister and a former policeman, Arkadii Gostev, who will have to manage almost 1,200 prisons and a budget of 4 billion euros, 1.5 per cent of the entire state expenditure (the highest percentage in Europe). About twenty other officials were dismissed, including the director of the Regional Tuberculosis Hospital Number 1 in Saratov and the director of the Irtkusk Prison, which was also at the centre of the scandal.

Kalashnikov's deputy Anatolii Yakunin is among those fired. Sergei tells me that he has never met Yakunin, but that he was the only high-ranking official to have tried to put a stop to systematic torture through several visits to prisons and meetings with victims and defence lawyers. 'Yakunin seemed genuinely sincere in wanting to reform the system and I'm sorry that an unwanted effect of my revelations was his firing.' The scandal dealt a severe blow to the FSB management of Russian prisons. Of course, change will be possible only if there is a decisive push from the president. At the 2021 end-of-the-year conference, Kseniya Sobchak – daughter of a late law professor and mayor of St Petersburg who had been a mentor to young Putin – had the courage to ask the president what he thought of the scandal. Putin replied: 'These tortures also take place in American and French prisons. Russian justice has opened seventeen investigations into the case and the guilty will be punished.' In July 2022 the parliament adopted a law that bans torture in prison; until then, prison guards could be charged only with abuse of power. Sergei tells me: 'There has been talk for at least ten years of a law on torture in prisons. It is certainly a positive sign that there is now a new impetus for it, thanks to our complaints.' But the present situation does not bode well for his own case. The Moscow prosecutor's office first opened an investigation into his conduct in relation to the dissemination of state secrets, then closed it. But, Sergei fears, more charges against him are on the way. The war in Ukraine has brought every reform to a standstill. Torture against Ukrainian civilians and captured military personnel during the 'special operation' are widespread. Since the beginning of the war in Ukraine, military authorities add this note to the file of soldiers who refuse to go to the front: 'Willing to use alcohol and drugs, commit thefts, and participate in anal orgies.' The last reference is a signal that, once in prison, these unfortunate individuals must be included in the caste of the untouchables.

When a regime approaches totalitarianism, even the mafias lose autonomy and are crushed, because the system does not tolerate any form of alternative power. For example, there is no mafia in North Korea. In Stalin's Russia, the brotherhood was almost entirely decimated. Large criminal associations thrive in democratic regimes, which fight organized crime without resorting to torture or summary executions. This is the price you pay for staying human. My mind goes back to my conversation with Sergei. 'Prison is a place that deforms the soul', he told me, and added – with difficulty, in a broken voice: 'In prison I lost my greatest human qualities, my sense of humour, trust in others, my naivety. I seem to have an emotional disability. I'm not sure I'll ever go back to who I was.' Such words reminded me of those written by Varlam Shalamov, who was confined to the Soviet Gulag in the 1930s and 1940s for sixteen years and went on to write *The Kolyma Tales*. In one short story, 'The typhoid quarantine', Shalamov describes his alter ego in these words: 'In his heart there was nothing but bitterness, and his spiritual wounds could not so easily be healed. They were never to heal.' The state of a country's prison is the moral test of a nation, of a people. Those who fail the test cannot call themselves civilized.

CHAPTER 4

THE CYBERCRIMINAL
NIKITA KUZMIN

In July 2010 the twenty-six-year-old Nikita Kuzmin is tour-ing Europe in a BMW 6 series convertible. As he stops to refuel, he writes to a friend that he is in love. As a show of affection for his girlfriend, he wants to buy her a photo shoot for *Playboy Russia*. A snapshot shows him smiling behind the wheel, with a trendy haircut and wearing a white polo shirt. His expression is enviably content. He is no longer the shy boy who grew up in the shadow of his stepfather's children. Nikita is experiencing a moment of grace: he is a respected millionaire in his virtual com-munity. Not only is he the inventor of Gozi, one of the most powerful viruses ever conceived, but he is also the creator of the organizational model of modern cybercrime, a model adopted by those who steal data to access online bank accounts as well as by those who engage in online extortion – a practice known as ransomware. Cybercrime-as-a-service has democratized internet crime and made it grow exponentially. The credit goes to Nikita.

The heroic era of cybercrime – the epoch when a brilliant youth, usually male, creates in his bedroom an invisible virus that infects computers all over the world – came to an end at the beginning of the twenty-first century. Today the system is made up of well-structured and specialized groups. The crime boss is the organizer of a business project; he may have some technical knowledge, but the coding is done by others. Cyberfraud requires diverse skills, which cannot all be present in one person. Gozi is the perfect example: this virus was conceived in 2005 by Kuzmin, who asked for help from the twenty-year-old Deniss 'Miami' Calovskis, born in Latvia but resident in Russia, and from the twenty-one-year-old Romanian Mihai Ionut Paunescu, known online by the nickname Virus. Nikita wanted to create the most powerful banking virus on record. He was the CEO, the visionary entrepreneur. Deniss was the genius programmer who wrote the codes, while Mihai managed the infected computers remotely. Other accomplices were hired for specific tasks: spammers who sent millions of emails and people who withdrew money in the victims' countries, especially in Europe and the United States. According to a recent study, 'there was also a manager who was paid $50,000 to $60,000 a year'. Nikita's group used the Jabber instant message system to communicate and its members spoke Russian. After months of work, the project was ready and the product could enter the market, competing with the powerful Zeus virus.

Gozi would arrive as a PDF document attached to an email. The unsuspecting recipient clicked on the PDF, believing it to be a legitimate document and, silently, the virus entered the computer and stole the victim's credentials, accessing their online bank accounts (never open an unsolicited attachment and never click on suspicious links remain the two best tips to protect yourself online). This information was transmitted to the owners of Gozi, who

then paid the attackers. Nikita and his men spent hours
making sure that the email message was written in perfect
English – for this they recruited translators on the dark web
– and that the attachments were credible. The time devoted
to this task was no shorter than the time devoted to writing
the codes. A fundamental technical innovation of Gozi was
to include a module (called hVNC) that allowed the hacker
to establish a direct and secret connection with the infected
computer. The criminal thus had access to all the victim's
data, for example their cookies or the websites they visited. This information was used together with the banking
credentials to empty the online account. Gozi ensured
total and imperceptible control of every infected machine.
Thus the hacker could sell all the information stored on the
machine about his victim, and not just steal their money.
For a while the account continued to appear on the screen
as normal and in the black, while in reality it had already
been emptied. Gozi has infected millions of computers and
is 'one of the most financially destructive computer viruses
in history', as declared in 2013 by Preet Bharara, the US
attorney for the Southern District of New York. American
and European customers and companies saw millions of
dollars disappear into thin air. This type of virus continues
to be the most requested one in criminal forums.

The division of labour paid off: for at least two years, Gozi
went completely undetected. In early 2007, when an analyst
suspected that something was wrong with a computer and
conducted a test, five out of seven of the most popular antivirus programs did not identify the Gozi file as suspicious.
Nikita had not just created a very powerful virus through
his criminal enterprise; he also laid the groundwork for
what was to become the standard organizational model of
twenty-first-century cybercrime. He called it '76 Service'

(that number was his nickname online). According to the model, the fraud is not carried out directly by the gang members, but they sell a service to customers with whom they communicate through a secure portal. In a chat from 2010, Nikita wrote to a potential client:

> NIKITA: Why do you need zeus, take my trojan [i.e. the Gozi virus]. Mine is much cooler, it doesn't get burned by proactives [i.e. a certain type of antivirus detection method] and works with win7 and vista [i.e. Windows and Vista operating systems].
>
> CUSTOMER: How much your trojan will cost me?
>
> NIKITA: 2k a month, including hosting and support. So you just have to upload [the virus]. I have the most convenient admin.

This figure of $2,000 represents a sum paid initially by those who carried out the attack. Once the affiliates demonstrated their capabilities, the team transitioned to full cybercrime-as-a-service mode, which had three components: the providers of technical tools (malicious code, servers, control panels); the suppliers of potential victims; and the performers who carried out the attack by exfiltrating money from bank accounts. This model envisions sharing profits equally, as one third goes to each group.

The service was personalized. The attacker indicated for example the bank he wanted to target, and Nikita created a team that wrote specific codes for that website and that particular credit institution. Service76 generated a customized version of Gozi, including the codes that were used to bypass the antivirus software. Finally it provided an infrastructure that would then be used by the hacker who bought Kuzmin's services to manage the hundreds of infected computers through a very easy to use point-and-click interface: it became possible to do it without difficulty – and to manipulate the interaction of victims with their banking institutions. The service also gave access to what is known as 'bulletproof hosting': secure sites where one could park the programs and everything they needed to implement the attacks. A division of Nikita's company was in charge of selecting and instructing the 'money mules' – usually Russians with tourist visas or students – to whom the funds stolen from foreign current accounts were transferred. Such people are called 'money mules' in the jargon. The transfer usually took place in two or three stages. The Gozi managers had control panels that tracked the transfers between accounts. The final extraction from the last group of mules – often located in the country where the criminals operated – could be done in various ways: through prepaid credit cards, through deposits into digital money accounts, by opening dedicated bank accounts, or via physical delivery.

The company generated fantastic profits, but disagreements soon emerged. It is also possible that Nikita thought he had earned enough cash. In any case, around 2009 he made a decision: 'I'm retiring.' And he put the company up for sale, as any successful entrepreneur would do. Nikita sold the codes to several customers, with an agreement that he should continue to receive a percentage of future profits. It is no coincidence that shortly afterwards he was travelling in a convertible BMW throughout Europe, fantasizing about his girlfriend naked in an issue of *Playboy*.

In September 2014 a report by the European Cybercrime Center concluded that the model inaugurated by Nikita had become an industry standard: the cybercrime industry is now a structured and commercialized business.

For example, the boss of the Evil Corp group, which specializes in cyber extortion (ransomware), stole around $100 million in more than forty countries, compromising at least eight companies on the *Forbes* 500 list. In keeping with the model inaugurated by Nikita in the early years of this century, Evil Corp was not the author of the operations, but sold the necessary tools to trusted customers – that is, cybercriminals who buy the service of the group. The cybercrime-as-a-service model produces innovation, solves complex problems, reduces risks, and generates large profits. Above all, the groups that create the viruses are not the same groups that spread them. The latter have almost no technical expertise and can be found in countries that are not those of the creators.

The Gozi gang operated in a vast ecosystem with many other parts, which facilitated its mission. As in so many other countries, in Russia too the criminal underground emerged in the 1990s, at the time of the birth of the internet. In this prehistoric phase, a small group of hackers found themselves on antediluvian chats – the so-called private bulletin boards (BBS) – where they discussed the best ways to download free writing software and data management programs. The discussions were chaotic and often ended in personal accusations and shouting. The next phase, which began in the late 1990s, was the creation of easily accessible forums on the internet. The first noteworthy Russian forum was HackZone.ru, which still exists today but has not been active for several years. An administrator organized traffic in the forum, but the topics covered were still too many. Forums soon specialized, some carrying out purely technical discussions, others focusing on particular activities such as stealing credit card numbers. And so Carder.org was born in 2000. Its site was well laid out, and any discussion that fell outside that particular type of fraud was banned. Several other sites specializing in credit card theft emerged later. The one best known today is called exploit.in. In 2019 exploit.in had more than 45,000 subscribers and reached an average of 1,300 comments per day. If you were in doubt about how to write a code, or on the lookout for a current account where you could deposit stolen money, this is where you'd find your answer. And if you were not satisfied with what you learned, you could switch to the Club2crd forum, where 120 thousand members are currently active. Entering these sites is easy, the administrators are nice, and some even operate in the clear on the web, so they can be found easily through Google. Others hide on the dark web, being accessible through the TOR program, which also ensures anonymity. By hiding on the dark web, visitors from other countries can avoid being identified by western police. In a study carried out a few years ago for TrendLabs, Max Goncharov found that no fewer than seventy-eight such forums were active in Russia. The authorities allow these sites to operate almost undisturbed, as long as the victims are not Russian citizens or institutions. Early in their careers, Nikita and his accomplices were very active on criminal forums, as they wanted to advertise Gozi and to sell 76 Service. Once the discussion got started, users moved on to fast and encrypted communication systems. The two most popular apps today are Telegram and, indeed, Jabber, the one also used by Nikita's group.

On criminal forums people go by their nickname. Nikita's was '76', which also became the brand for his product. It is essential for any criminal to build a reputation as a trustworthy person, with whom others can make credible deals. In this world, such a reputation is all contained in the name used online. This is why no one can afford to have their virtual identity tarnished. Sometimes, however, these individuals are forced to change their nickname in order to avoid being identified by the authorities, and therefore risk losing the 'reputational capital' accumulated by their brand name. One hacker was so upset at the prospect of changing his nickname that he wrote in a forum: 'Here my name is solv3nt, but in other forums I am known by the name of dentrino.' In this way he was trying not to lose the credibility accumulated in the past.

Each forum has a section reserved for trusted members. To access it, you have to go through a fairly rigorous screening. Apart from recommendations and sometimes the request to take an admission test, a fundamental criterion is the knowledge of Russian. The FBI has several analysts proficient in the language, usually Americans born in the Soviet Union, but often they are unable to answer questions about recent TV programs or everyday life. They are quickly smoked out as residents in the States trying to pass themselves off as citizens of today's Russia.

A fascinating aspect of Russian underground forums is the emergence of a special language, which uses English terms but russifies them. For example, a 'keylogger' (the act of identifying what a person types on a computer keyboard) becomes килогер (*kiloger*) – instead of the more correct 'keyboard spy', клавиатурный шпион (*klaviaturnyi shpion*), which exists in technical jargon). The Jabber communication system becomes *Zhaba* (Жаба). In some cases, ordinary words take on a special meaning. Two of the best known and most iconic nouns in this world are *karton* and *kartofel*. In current Russian, the first means 'paper box' and the second 'potato', while in criminal language both mean 'credit card'. Paypal becomes *palka*, which literally means 'stick'. As much as an outside analyst can learn this jargon, it changes all the time and making mistakes is easy.

In addition to the forums where the criminals meet, discuss, and plan attacks, in Russia there are dozens of sites organized like Amazon.com, where one can buy goods of all kinds without having to interact with anyone. While forum discussions can go on for weeks and end in stalemate, here transactions are standardized and payments are strictly in bitcoin. These illegal sites, born around 2010, have seen an exponential growth since around 2013.

The most famous one was the Russian Anonymous Marketplace, which operated from 2012 until 2017 – a very long time in this world. Its creator, known only by his nickname, DarkSide, had banned all political propaganda, as well as the sale of weapons and pornography, and customers had to be Russian. The site closed down in 2017 as a result of an autonomous decision taken by the new administrators, and not thanks to an intervention by the authorities. (Rumour had it that the administrators defrauded some customers, but there is no solid evidence.)

This virtual marketplace was soon replaced by Hydra Market, which has more than 1,740 specialized areas and where drugs, fake IDs, counterfeit money and almost all kinds of digital merchandise are sold. The site has grown by 640 per cent over the past three years and, according to an estimate, controls 75 per cent of the market, with transactions worth $1.37 billion (in bitcoin) in 2020 – a result achieved in the middle of the pandemic. Hydra Market, which is located on the dark web, was born as a portal for the sale of drugs, but soon diversified to other products. Managed by eleven administrators, it also offers a job search service with almost 2,000 offers at the moment. A particularly sought-after role is that of *KladMan* (literally 'treasure man' or 'treasurer'), namely a person who drops drugs or cash in designated physical places, in airtight envelopes that can be recovered by the client, as a recent report by the Flashpoint Research Center explained.

In short, Hydra has introduced a pioneering Uber cybercrime service: the goods arrive wherever you want, without going through the post office or a private courier, both of which are unreliable, even if for different reasons. To reduce the risk of infiltration by foreign police officers, those who sell on Hydra can cash out their proceeds only after completing fifty transactions and must maintain an account of no less than $10,000 on the site. Several studies have shown that prices for illegal goods and services have dropped significantly over the past decade. The market is highly competitive, and the services offered are of excellent quality.

The Russian criminal underground has another unique feature. Dozens of sites sell confidential information. Many analysts have pointed out that the level of accuracy of the data collected there is extraordinary. You can order detailed files on a person wherever they are, and obtain their passport information, photos, marriage history, international travel data, surveillance video recordings, extradition requests, property deeds, professional history, and more. The site to follow for this kind of information is called Probiv (from a Russian noun that means 'search'). In 2019 Probiv had more than 50,000 discussion topics and 41,000 subscribers. The dossiers Probiv offers contain telephone calls and the geolocation of the person surveilled. It is also possible to buy fake passports, certificates, and university degrees on this site. Probiv is the ideal supermarket for resource-strapped spy agencies, but also for

jealous partners and competitors. American clients have
been found on Probiv.

There is a dangerous analytical trap into which many
observers fall. They think that cybercrime activities take
place exclusively in the virtual sphere. Instead there is also
an important *offline* dimension to cybercrime, made up of
face-to-face meetings that occur in a physical place. For
example, the central members of Nikita's group knew one
another personally. At one point during an intercepted conversation in 2010, Nikita wrote: 'Well, let's meet in person
and let's talk about it.' Some countries tolerate cybercrime
more than others, and it is therefore easier to meet in a cafe
or a restaurant in Moscow than in New York.

In fact cyberattacks are not evenly distributed around
the world. For historical and political reasons, some
countries are nerve centres of cybercrime. According
to a report by the Center for Strategic and International
Studies (CSIS), during the period 2006–18, at least 108
significant attacks were launched from China (here 'significant' means that these attacks have cost more than $1
million each). In this ranking the third place goes to Iran,
which is followed by North Korea and India. According
to Kaspersky Lab, 23.52 per cent of the spam emails sent
between July and September 2020 originated from Russia
– the first country in this ranking. Offering an accurate
explanation of these lists is a complex task. In some cases
there are historical reasons. For example, the Romanian
dictator Nicolai Ceausescu promoted his country's
internet connectivity and the study of computer science
in the 1980s. When the regime ended, there were many
computer-savvy young people in Romania – a country
that is well connected to the internet but at the same time
is rather poor. Romania thus became an important centre

of internet fraud related to the sale of fictitious goods in the European Union.

The picturesque town of Râmnicu Vâlcea, located 179 kilometres north-east of Bucharest, was nicknamed Hackerville by *Wired* magazine in 2011 (in 2018 HBO produced a television series of the same title dedicated to Râmnicu Vâlcea). Specialized gangs were able to rob hundreds of customers who wanted to rent vacation homes or buy goods on eBay. Several corrupt policemen and politicians were arrested in Râmnicu Vâlcea precisely because they were protecting some of these gangs. Perhaps it is no coincidence that Mihai, Nikita's alleged accomplice, was born in Romania. The local and *offline* dimension allows cybercrime to thrive online. This tolerance makes it possible for cybercrime to evolve and become extremely sophisticated, similar in all respects to a legal industry.

In Russia, cybercrime gangs operate relatively unpunished, as long as they respect certain basic rules and, when necessary, help to promote the country's strategic interests. Russia hit the headlines in 2016 because it was accused of sanctioning the hacking of a huge collection of US Democratic Party emails during the election campaign. According to western sources, a group known as APT29 was responsible for the attack. In addition to penetrating the sites of the Democrats and the Pentagon, APT29 has also conducted intrusions into the sites of the Norwegian Ministry of Foreign Affairs, the British Labour Party, and the Dutch Ministry of Defence as well as into official portals in Germany and South Korea. Together with APT28 – a similar group that specializes in operations against countries and organizations in the Caucasus and at NATO – it is capable of spreading viruses that are very difficult to detect. Both APT29 and APT28 create tailor-made programs for a specific attack, so they require a significant commitment of resources. According to IntSights analysts, the two groups are a direct offshoot of the Russian secret services (FSB and SVR). It is no coincidence that the FBI placed two Russian army officers on the list of most wanted cybercriminals and, in 2018, formally accused seven officials of the Armed Forces Information Service (GRU) of conducting attacks on American official sites. It is strongly suspected that the Sandworm Team, created in 2009 and specializing in actions against Ukraine, is also linked to the Russian army, even if it seems less sophisticated than APT29 and APT28 (western services are, obviously, no less active in their attacks on sites in Russia and in other non-friendly countries). Yet the type of relationship between cybercrime and the authorities is not symbiosis. When asked, hackers are willing to help. Once the task is done, they return to their main profession. The Gozi group itself has been accused by US authorities of having compromised about sixty NASA computers.

Political protection is invaluable. In early 2021, a group known as Bugatti, which had been infiltrated by the American authorities, was heavily criticized in a forum on the dark web. The messages accused Bugatti of recruiting non-Russian members and thus exposing itself to FBI infiltration. Bugatti, which specialized in online extortion, also made the mistake of keeping some servers out of Russia. 'Mother Russia will help you. Love your country, and nothing will happen to you!' reads a message of criticism intercepted by the information security company Advanced Intelligence. Nonetheless, there is no evidence that Russian government agencies receive material benefits from cybercrime. They simply turn a blind eye and ask for help when needed.

In Russia, despite the presence of an underground cyber network that has no equivalent in the world for complexity and sophistication, the government's control over the internet is draconian. In every internet service provider, the authorities have installed programs that give them direct access to users' data without having to seek permission from a judge. The system, which is called SORM, is provided by the security services. The new version, SORM 3, increases the government's ability to monitor, collect, filter, and store a wide range of data concerning the online behaviour of Russian citizens. The recent Digital Sovereignty Law, issued in 2019, allows the government to disconnect all users from the internet, and hence to erect a great wall between the country and the rest of the world. Authorities say that this law is necessary insofar as it protects the internet from foreign attacks aimed at disconnecting the country.

The life of anti-Putin hackers is difficult. The best known group is a Russian version of Anonymous. This version is called Anonymous International and was created by the opposition journalist Vladimir Anikeev. Active at least since 2013, it is famous also under the name Shaltai Boltai, which is the Russian for Humpty Dumpty. In 2014 and 2015 it hacked the prime minister's Twitter account and several other official sites. Anikeev was arrested in 2016 and the group has been inactive ever since. Another group is known as Ovirus. This one has been luckier so far, as it was able in 2019 to steal about 7.5 terabytes of data from Russian news agencies; but it is likely that the attack originated in a third country.

How can cybercrime be effectively combated? A study published by the Third Way institute in 2018 concluded that the probability of arresting perpetrators of cyberattacks is three in a thousand. For ransomware attacks, the chance of success is even lower. A typical strategy of the American authorities is to block access to forums or sites for buying and selling illegal goods. This happened in a sensational way with the closure of the online black market Silk Road in 2013 and the confiscation of $1 billion in bitcoin. An official note from the FBI was telling those who wanted to visit this internet address that the site has been seized. The police put the computer equivalent of seals on the entrance door to a crime scene.

The authorities arrest the perpetrators as soon as they can, as in any other investigation. But this is not always the best strategy. In any case, it has no chance of success when the server and the culprits are in a country that, for geopolitical reasons, has no intention of cooperating. A group of researchers from the universities of Cambridge and Oxford recently suggested strategies that do not involve closing the site or shutting it down. The idea is to undermine the reputation of sellers and buyers of illegal goods on the dark web. The two proposed strategies are (1) posting false feedback regarding the quality of the purchased goods, and (2) creating fictitious identities of defective merchandise suppliers, although undercover agents leave positive feedback. The research group has already begun conducting virtual experiments designed to test whether these two strategies are effective. The preliminary findings are encouraging. In the presence of these strategies, sellers are forced to reduce the quality and value of the goods sold. The most successful mechanism consists in spreading unfounded rumours about the reliability of the sellers. So, in addition to trying to arrest criminals and shut down sites, western police can adopt more subtle tactics, such as inserting doses of distrust into illegal exchanges.

This approach hurts even those who work in jurisdictions where cybercrime is tolerated.

Once he managed to sell his company, Nikita decided to explore the wide world, like Faust in Goethe's tragedy. In June 2010 he was in Switzerland, at the World Cup match between Switzerland and Honduras, which ended nil–nil. The Swiss team played poorly and did not qualify. 'There was such a tragedy here', Nikita told a friend. At the end of July he was still travelling around Europe in his new convertible car. A friend wrote to him asking what he had done with the Audi. 'Audi was in the winter, the convertible in the summer.' He posted some photos of his travels on the Russian site YouDo, where he had a profile. He had a second profile, too, on the Russian version of Facebook.

Here one could also find his email address, which could be easily hacked. It seems that Nikita had forgotten a cardinal rule of his world: the more you share online, the more vulnerable you become. He began to believe that he was invincible and did not suspect that he had become a target for the American authorities. So he made mistakes. For example, while traveling to Europe, he confirmed his bank account number to a customer using a non-secure link, and thus providing direct evidence of his illegal activities. In November he moved to Bangkok and, after spending almost a month in Thailand, he made a decision that was to cost him his freedom: on 27 November he flew to San Francisco, where he hoped to attend a computer conference. Several reports also suggest that he had invested in a variety of US internet companies and wanted to visit them. In any case, as soon as he set foot on American soil, he was arrested. The prosecution asked for ninety-five years of imprisonment. Nikita followed his lawyer's advice – the same lawyer will represent Trump's son in 2016, in the

investigation into Russian cyberattacks on the Democratic
Party emails – and decided to collaborate: he revealed the
names of his two main accomplices and the entire structure of the operational model of 76 Service. Mihai Ionut
Paunescu was arrested in Romania in 2012, with the prospect of spending sixty-five years in jail, but the Romanian
judges refused to extradite him and he vanished into thin
air. Deniss Calovskis, the Gozi programmer, was captured
in Latvia, on charges that could have cost him sixty-seven
years in an American prison. Sent to the United States, he
pleaded guilty and spent twenty-one months in jail.

While awaiting trial, Nikita was able to access the internet, update his Facebook photo, and even (allegedly) attend
an official Kremlin event online. Nikita's collaboration was
repaid by the American authorities and, in 2016, he was
sentenced to compensate some of the victims to the sum of
6.9 million dollars, and his detention was shortened to the
time he had already served. He was a free man again. After
a brief return to Russia, where he lived in Saint Petersburg
working as a designer and managed some online trading
platforms, he moved abroad again. Meanwhile, American
justice was still on the lookout for the other members of
the Gozi gang. In the summer of 2021, a man between thirty
and forty years, with a thick beard and a red T-shirt, was
seen wandering around the streets of Bogotá. After a brief
investigation, it turned out that the man was Mihai. When
he tried to leave the Colombian capital on 29 June, he was
arrested. After more than one year in a Colombian jail,
he was extradited to the United States, where he pleaded
guilty and, on 12 June 2023, was sentenced to three years in
prison by the Manhattan federal court.

In the meantime Gozi has morphed into a thousand vari-
ants and leads a life of its own, disconnected from that of

its creators. Nikita's plan to sell the codes and to continue to benefit from them didn't work. Soon after the sale, the buyers were themselves hacked and the codes surfaced on the dark web. The best banking virus ever created has gone public. The analytical structure of the first version of Gozi is now present in almost all programs used to steal data. The new Gozis have names such as Gozi Prinimalka, Gozi ISFB, Gozi CRM, Schnitzel Gozi, Goziv3, Neverquest, Rovnix, Vawtrack, Tepfer, Dapato, Ursnif, and many more. An article published by CheckPoint Research in August 2020 is rightly entitled 'Gozi: Malware with a Thousand Faces'. Nikita, who now changed his life, got married, and started travelling again, has wrapped us in a spider's web that doesn't break easily.

CONCLUSIONS

What do these four stories tell us – and what do they fail to tell us – about the bigger picture of Russia's transformations from the 1980s to the present? In the late Soviet period the state began to loosen its control over the economy, which led to the reforms introduced by Gorbachev from 1985 onwards. During that time the cooperative movement and the first embryonic private enterprises emerged. But markets do not self-regulate. Simply liberalizing the economy is not enough; it is necessary to build a framework of laws and administrative structures to resolve conflicts among owners. Gorbachev's reform project was unable to create the legal framework that markets require, and professional criminals already operating in the informal economy of the 1970s partially took on the role that should belong to the state.

First the rudimentary gang of the Mongol, and then the much more sophisticated one of Ivan'kov, carved out a governance role in the emerging market economy. The value of privatized assets was astronomical and other groups, such as the Chechens and Azerbaijanis, wanted to participate in the division of the spoils, thus beginning the Great Mob War of the 1990s. The Russian mafia was then in effect replacing the state and fighting for its survival.

One would have hoped that the first democratically elected president of Russia, Boris Yeltsin, had succeeded where Gorbachev had failed. Instead, the political elite that took the reins of the country in the 1990s was far from being a fair third-party enforcer of contracts and antitrust principles. It was not an honest broker: rather it engaged in a ruthless struggle with other elements of the old Soviet system to gain control of the economy and re-create in Russia the authoritarian regime undermined by Gorbachev's reforms. People like George, whom I met in Perm in the 1990s, could survive only if they had a powerful protector within the political system or the support of the mafia. This was the opposite of the rule of law. Turf wars were now occurring at all levels of the system, not just among small gangs. The West committed the serious mistake of not recognizing the violent nature of the project from the outset. Clinton's congratulatory phone call to Yeltsin sealed the West's support for the state model that would later become Putin's. Boris Berezovsky was a quintessential figure of this period. As an astute individual positioned at the edges of the Soviet power structure, he adeptly navigated the tumultuous 1990s, ultimately winning Yeltsin's favour. Berezovsky seized the opportunity to enrich himself while continuing to assist Yeltsin in the destruction of the nascent democracy. He defrauded the Russian public and yet was never sanctioned. Together with other oligarchs, he played dirty to ensure Yeltsin's re-election in 1996. Cheating in the market game goes hand in hand with undermining democratic values. As a rule, bullies and plunderers do not promote the birth of a system that will devalue their skills.

On the eve of another presidential election, in September 1999, tragedy struck: a series of explosions targeted residential buildings in the Russian cities of Buinaksk, Moscow, and Volgodonsk. More than three hundred people died and more than a thousand were injured. Fear spread across Russia. On 23 September, the day after a fourth attack was attempted but failed, Yeltsin signed a decree that triggered the Second Chechen War. Berezovsky was complicit in the launch of that operation. Vladimir Putin, the Russian prime minister at the time, saw a boost in his popularity that contributed to his rise to the presidency within months. Several observers, including Anna Politkovskaya, thought that the 1999 terrorist attacks were instigated by state authorities close to Yeltsin to help Putin win. This strategy aimed to guarantee that the corrupt agreements that were in place at the time would be upheld at the next stage in the nation's political history. So Yeltsin and his entourage would escape prison. David Satter, then a *Wall Street Journal* journalist in Moscow, has subsequently written that Berezovsky must have been involved in the planning of the bombings.

The new president, Vladimir Putin, chose to destabilize the economic system and the property rights acquired by the oligarchs – the main industrialists of the previous decade – because such a pattern of ownership would have provided a platform from which it was possible to launch an attack on him. Surely the privatization had been unfair. But Putin aimed to undo its outcome by replacing one cadre with another. Injecting uncertainty is a mechanism of control. Nobody's property and life were safe. This is how Berezovsky fell out of favour and fled to London.

Of course, Russia also modernized, at least until around 2012. Thanks to high oil prices, GDP grew from $13,000 in 1999 to $24,000 in 2011, and average salaries and pensions increased by about 11 per cent in real terms. In 2000, one in forty-eight people had a contract for a mobile phone, while eleven years later there were almost two mobile phones per individual. In 2012, three quarters of families had a computer. Russians became more educated and travelled abroad regularly. Changes in consumption, media, and internet usage, the rise in education, and integration into international markets began to make Russia an advanced country with post-industrial features, although significant disparities between the centre and the periphery persisted.

And yet economic prosperity did not reduce widespread illegality. According to data collected by Indem, a Moscow-based research institute, the real value of bribes increased nearly tenfold between 2001 and 2005. Russia's corruption index remained essentially unchanged from 1996 to 2021. According to 2022 calculations, a company pays in the region of 22.5 percent of the public contract in bribes. Almost everything is up for sale.

Widespread illegality unleashed demands for the rule of law and democracy in the now relatively affluent population. Russians began to protest. Millions signed online petitions on the Change.org platform, World Wildlife Fund Russia became very popular for its battles against environmental disasters, such as oil spills, and Aleksei Navalny's anti-corruption campaigns were relentless. In the autumn of 2011, crowds of citizens across Russia disputed the result of the parliamentary election, which had been blatantly rigged in favour of Putin's party. The return to the presidency, in 2012, of the man 'with winter eyes' sparked another massive wave of dissent, known as 'the

Bolotnaya Square protests'. At the same time GDP began to contract from 2013 onwards, and by 2015 inflation was at 13 per cent. For the first time since 1999, real incomes declined.

Putin believed that a shift towards the rule of law and democracy would unhorse him; and he was not sure he could keep his wealth and freedom in a post-Putin Russia. Hence he reacted by accusing the United States of interfering in the country's internal politics and by introducing a series of repressive measures. He passed a law that limited the activities of 'foreign agents', a term borrowed from the Cold War that now includes newspapers, television, websites, NGOs, and Russian citizens who disseminate information. In 2013 any 'propaganda' in favour of gay causes was prohibited. In 2016 the law on extremism and terrorism was amended to make internet control easier. In the same year, freedom of worship as practised by religious organizations not recognized by the state was restricted. The following year saw a law decriminalizing domestic violence.

Putin inaugurated a mini cult of his personality and developed an ideology based on media manipulation, aggressive nationalism, the attack of the West, the myth of the fight against Nazism culminating in the victory of the Second World War, and a generic nostalgia for the Soviet Union (its disintegration had been a 'geopolitical catastrophe', the president declared in April 2005).

Even the semblance of legality was lost, albeit gradually. Increasingly, the word of the dictator is law, as theorized by Andrei Klishas – jurist, senator, and prominent member of the party United Russia. In an interview with the newspaper *Vedomosti* on 8 December 2022, he stated: 'From the point of view of legitimacy, in our country there is nothing that has greater force than the word of the president . . . Do you think that a decree has more force than his word? I don't think so and, in any case, it doesn't in the perception of the people.' The jurists of the Third Reich would have no difficulty in recognizing the *Führerprinzip* in today's Russia.

The war in Ukraine in 2022 – the largest land conflict in Europe since the Second World War – was also motivated by domestic repression. War abroad allows increasing pressure within the country. If Ukraine were to offer Russians a model of western democracy, the regime would be in danger. Putin's nightmare almost came true in 2011, when Russians massively protested against frauds in the parliamentary elections. The invasion of Donbas and the annexation of Crimea in 2014 occurred after the Euromaidan protests, leading to the flight of the pro-Russian Ukrainian president Yanukovych and the free elections of 2014. For many scholars, the question of NATO expansion (invoked as the cause of Putin's military adventures in Europe) is a card played when it's convenient to suppress pushes for freedom at home.

Is the Putinist model stable? One must not under-estimate the weapon Putin employs: fear. Totalitarian regimes are built on fear, as explained by Hannah Arendt. Twentieth-century dictators disposed of faithful servants and opponents. Everybody lives in fear: your neighbour, the believer genuflecting beside you, or your schoolmate could inform on you and be responsible for your demise. For example Ioann Burdin, the priest of the small village of Karabanovo in central Russia, was reported on 6 March 2022 by a worshiper who listened to his sermon. There are no safe places, not even in the house of God. Therefore the wisest strategy for those who want to survive in this inverted world is isolation, silence, and deception. The dictator wants to create a 'completely isolated human being', and 'the most elementary caution requires avoiding all intimate contacts', as Arendt wrote. Fear of fellow citizens is the engine that allows the system to function, making grassroots collective action very difficult to achieve. Many, of course, leave the country to avoid submission. Hidden under the oppression of totalitarian power, freedom always resists, but the ways, times, and outcomes of such resistance are difficult to predict today.

The macro history of Russia intertwines with the micro history recounted in this book. Olga Romanova, the financial journalist who founded the association Russia behind Bars in 2008, after her husband's arrest, and now lives in Berlin, points to 2014–15 as the year when the order to quash the thieves in law in prison was given. Mass rapes were punishment for those who did not comply: mostly ordinary convicts and professional criminals. What Sergei Savel'ev uncovered is irrefutable evidence. The death in custody of Alexei Navalny on 16 February 2024, at the age of forty-seven, is further proof that Putin's neo-Gulags are tools of political terror.

The regime, however, has vulnerabilities that are not evident to everyone.

The story of Nikita Kuzmin is exemplary. Russia imports technology, but the state apparatus, including the security services, is corrupt and inefficient. Its members are thus forced to turn to freelance criminals to carry out their operations. In this way they allow cybercriminals to operate with impunity, as long as they do not attack the Russian state and people. There is more. The war in Ukraine in 2022 may have additional unintended effects that led to the further weakening of the system. The economy is kept alive by state military spending, while the civilian economy is suffering, together with the disposable income and the retail sales. The prices of essential goods have gone up. Cash-strapped Russians are increasingly turning to loan sharks to make ends meet. Since early March 2022, dollar accounts have been closed, entrepreneurs are forced to convert foreign earnings into roubles, and strict controls on capital export have come into effect. Thus the black market for currency exchange has exploded. Dozens of illegal Telegram chats connect buyers and sellers of currency. The economy is increasingly escaping state control. Stockbrokers interviewed by Bloomberg report that many of them buy and sell stocks by phone, outside official channels, and can be robbed or extorted by unscrupulous individuals. The most significant criminals of the 1990s, such as Ivan'kov, cut their teeth in the informal economy of the preceding decade. Even in Russia observers have started to ask whether 'the wild 1990s' are back.

The criminalization of state and society may go even further than in the 1990s. The sanctions imposed on Russia force many economic and military sectors to use illegal channels to circumvent them. The process extends from the systematic use of accounts in tax havens to the sale of gold on the black market and to the purchase of technology and weapons through the network of post-Soviet mafiosi who reside outside Russia's borders – in Georgia, Armenia, Kyrgyzstan, Uzbekistan, and Greece.

Because of the war, the timid initiatives to increase transparency in procurement and to sign international treaties against corruption have been repudiated. Police are busy arresting protesters; thus resources are diverted from the fight against ordinary crime. In the meantime, a thriving market for fake medical certificates and diplomas used to avoid conscription has emerged. Several friends of mine have offered bribes to spare their children from going to Ukraine.

We may have come full circle. In 1994, when I was a student, I wrote an essay titled "Is Sicily the Future of Russia?". The situation in the early 1990s presents eerie parallels with the factors that led to the emergence of the Sicilian mafia in the nineteenth century. In southern Italy, a rapid yet deeply flawed transition to capitalism went unaccompanied by any clear definition and protection of property rights. At the same time there was an abundance of people trained in the use of violence who could not find legitimate employment after the defeat of the Bourbon army. The combination of these factors led to the emergence of the Sicilian mafia. This argument was put forward by my DPhil supervisor, Diego Gambetta. I could see that the transition to capitalism in Russia in the 1990s was also rapid and flawed. Reductions in the ranks of the police and the army, the release of prisoners, and the lack of opportunities for veterans of the Afghan War (1978–88) generated a supply of people ready to enter illegality. At the same time, people like George were cutting their teeth in the market and needed protection for deals and property. Demand met supply. It was the perfect storm.

Can this process happen again? In the 2020s, many battle-hardened soldiers, some directly recruited from prison, will come back to the cities of Russia with few employment opportunities and ready to join the underworld. Without fail, they will bring back weapons that will end up in the black market (indeed, crimes involving firearms have increased in the country since 2022). It is not unlikely that a myriad of associations of former combatants would spring up as a result of receiving favourable tax breaks to import goods, as happened in the 1990s. Like before, this is a recipe for such organizations to become criminalized. The mafias that Putin thought he had defeated would acquire unexpected strength. At the same time, if the war in Ukraine is lost, a change of political class could occur, unleashing a wave of reforms.

Russia seems to be caught in a vicious circle of liberalization, chaos, and repression. Those who, like me, care about the fate of this wonderful country and its people hope that Russia's past will not be its destiny.

NOTES AND FURTHER READINGS

Notes to Introduction

A classic overview of the transition to the market in Russia is David E. Hoffman, *The Oligarchs: Wealth and Power in the New Russia* (Public Affairs: New York 2003). Most relevant is the chapter on Berezovsky. See also my book: Federico Varese, *The Russian Mafia: Private Protection in a New Market Economy* (Oxford University Press: Oxford 2001), especially ch. 1 (pp. 17–36). An in-depth account of Putin's regime is Robert Service, *Kremlin Winter: Russia and the Second Coming of Vladimir Putin* (Picador: London 2020). See also Maria Chiara Franceschelli, 'La storia è il futuro: Il presente è senza storia', *il Mulino*, 2 (2022), pp. 149–56.

2 **At that time inflation**   Visit https://www.statbureau .org/en/russia/inflation/1994. For the whole year, the inflation rate in Russia was 215.02 per cent, which was 624.85 percentage points lower than the rate in 1993.

5 **predictability and equality**   See Stephen Holmes, 'Lineages of the rule of law', in Adam Przeworski and José María Maravall (eds), *Democracy and the Rule of Law* (Cambridge University Press: Cambridge 2003), p. 20.

5 **Habermas**   See Jürgen Habermas, 'On the internal relation between the rule of law and democracy', *European Journal of Philosophy* 3(1), 1995, p. 13.

8 **The four stories told in this book teach us**   The view that Russian democracy lasted only for a brief period of time is a topic touched upon by several scholars.

Bengt Jangfeldt, *L'Idea russa: Da Dostoevskij a Putin* (Neri Pozza: Vicenza 2022, p. 130) suggests that it did not extend beyond the period 1991–3. See also Peter Reddaway and Dmitri Glinski, *The Tragedy of Russia's Reforms: Market Bolshevism against Democracy* (United States Institute of Peace Press: Washington, DC 2000), p. 371.

9 **Towards the end of my stay** *The God that Failed*, edited by Richard Crossman (Hamish Hamilton: London 1950), is a collection of essays by authors such as Arthur Koestler, Ignazio Silone, and André Gide on the horrors of Stalinism.

Notes to Chapter 1

11 **as I narrate in my book *Mafia Life*** See Federico Varese, *Mafia Life: Life, Death and Money at the Heart of Organized Crime* (Profile: London 2017), pp. 209–12.

11 **the man who coached the Russian national hockey team** This is Viktor Tíkhonov. The author of Ivankov's tomb is the artist Aleksándr Rukavíshnikov.

12 **the deceased's religiosity** See Varese, *Russian Mafia*, p. 185.

12–14 **Born in Moscow on 2 January 1940** The information I give here on Ivan'kov's life comes from the following sources: Nikolai Modestov, *Moskva Banditskaya* [*Criminal Moscow*] (Tsentrloligrag: Moscow 1996), pp. 258–75; Andrei Kostantinov, *Banditskii Peterburg* [*Criminal Petersburg*] (Folio Press: St Petersburg 1997), pp. 75–93; Aleksei Maximov, *Rossiiskaya Prestupnost': Kto est' Kto* [*Criminal Russia: Who's Who*] (Izdatel'stvo 'Eksmo': Moscow 1997), pp. 361–71; Vyacheslav Razinkin and Aleksei Tarabrin, *Tsvetnaya mast': Elita prestupnogo mira* [*Those Who Follow the Code: The Elite of the Criminal World*] (Veche: Moscow 1997); and Evgenii Snegov, '"Krestnyi otets" sovetskoy prestupnosti: Istoriya Yaponchika, odnogo iz samykh izvestnykh vorov v zakone' ['The

"Godfather" of Soviet crime: The story of Yaponchik, one of the most famous thieves in law'], *Secretmag*, 29.10.2021, https://secretmag.ru/criminal/istoriya-yap onchika.htm. In English, a most valuable source is Robert E. Friedman, *Red Mafiya: How the Russian Mob Invaded America* (Little, Brown: Boston, MA 2000), pp. 108–17, 119–39.

13 **Yet we may want to exercise a degree of caution over this diagnosis** I am grateful to Judith Pallot for reminding me of this fact. Schizophrenia was a rather loose concept in Soviet psychiatry and was also used for political purposes. See Richard J. Bonnie and Svetlana V. Polubinskaya, 'Unraveling Soviet psychiatry', *Journal of Contemporary Legal Issues* 10, 1999, pp. 279–98.

15 **the average gross salary** Data on average gross monthly salary in 1981 come from http://opoccuu.com /wages.htm. Slightly different figures can be found at https://45-90.ru/articles/srednemesjachnye-zarabot nye-platy-s-1960-po-2001-g.html (178.3 rouble) and at https://top-rf.ru/investitsii/581-srednyaya-zarplata .html (168.9 rouble, but only for 1980: the figure for 1981 is missing).

15 **proto-mafia** For a discussion on the definition of organized crime and mafia, see Federico Varese, 'What is organised crime?', in Federico Varese (ed.), *Organised Crime: Critical Concepts in Criminology* (Routledge: London 2010), vol. 1, pp. 11–33.

15 **Two bullets ended up in the body of a Georgian** The Georgian boss wounded by Ivan'kov in 1974 was Goga Dgebuadze (Goga Tbilisskii).

15–18 **At its apex was a brotherhood of leaders known as *vory v zakone*** Here I draw upon Varese, *Russian Mafia*, pp. 145–86 and Varese, *Mafia Life*, pp. 17–22.

16 **A French citizen convicted as a spy** The French citizen condemned as a spy by the Soviets was Maximilien de Santerre (see Varese, *Russian Mafia*, pp. 145–6).

16 **A similar split**   On the attitude of the *vory* fraternity
to the 2022 war, see Federico Varese, 'L'editto della
mafia russa: "Sulla guerra in Ucraina siamo neutrali"',
Repubblica, 26 June 2022 and Zhanna Ulyanova, 'Mafiya
gibnet za Putina: Geografiya prestupnogo mira Rossii,
predstavlennaya na fronte' ['The mafia is dying for Putin:
Geography of the Russian underworld present at the
front'], 19 June 2023, https://www.poligon.media/mafi
ya-gibnet-za-putina. On the historical split, see Federico
Varese, 'The society of the vory-v-zakone, 1930s–1950s',
Cahiers du monde russe (1998), pp. 515–38.

17 **Avoid any conflict**   Quotation from Varese, *Mafia Life*,
p. 17; translation slightly modified.

18 **eight-pointed star**   Next to the eight-pointed star, the
so-called 'hussar epaulettes' is also a distinctive mark of
the *vory*. On the symbolism of the eight-pointed star, see
e.g. Jack Tresidder, *Symbols and their Meanings* (Duncan
Baird: London 2006). The online site of New York's
Metropolitan Museum of Art has detailed articles and
images related to the eight-pointed star in various cultures; visit https://www.metmuseum.org.

19 **I hate luxury**   Ivan'kov's words on luxury are cited
in Maksim Kal'kovskii, 'Yaponchik: Pravda ob ottse
rossiiskoi mafii', *Globalist*, 10 August 2009, https://
globalist.org.ua/novosti/society-news/yaponchik-
biografiya-no18790.html.

19 **His lawyer**   Ivan'kov's lawyer in 1981 was Heinrich
Padva. His statements are quoted in the 29 October 2021
issue of the magazine *Secretmag*.

20 **A fellow thief in law who was in the same prison
recounted the following**   The prisoner who recounts
Ivan'kov's role in Tulun Prison in his memoirs is *vor*
Leonid Semikolenov. The text can be found at https://
www.primecrime.ru.

21 **a prominent Soviet-era singer**   The singer who signed
the petition was Iosif Kobzon, together with the future

candidate in the 1996 elections, the ophthalmologist Svyatoslav Federov. See Varese, *Russian Mafia*, p. 182.

21 **The Russia of 1991**   Paul Klebnikov, *Godfather of the Kremlin: Boris Berezovsky and the Looting of Russia* (Harcourt: San Diego, CA 2000), p. 25. Paul Klebnikov was murdered in 2004, in Moscow, for his work as an investigative journalist.

23 **'Superpower'**   See Candice Hughes, 'Yeltsin: Russia a "Superpower of Crime"', Associated Press, 7 June 1994.

24–5 **the Great Mob War**   See Klebnikov, *Godfather of the Kremlin*, pp. 11–45.

25 **deaths of the members of the brotherhood**   On average, 9.6 thieves in law died per year in the period 1970–9, by comparison to 21.7 per year in the period 1980–9 and 56.7 per year in the period 1990–9. Data come from Federico Varese, Jakub Lonsky, and Yuriy Podvysotskiy, 'The resilience of the Russian mafia: An empirical study', *British Journal of Criminology*, 61(1), 2021, pp. 143–66.

25 **The Brotherhood of the Sun**   This section draws upon Varese, *Mafias on the Move*, p. 106 and Varese, *Mafia Life*, p. 106.

25 **In an FBI report from 1995**   See Varese, *Mafias on the Move*, pp. 66–7.

26 **All the criminal activities of the Sointsevskaya**   Quoted from Varese, *Mafia Life*, 106.

26 **Two versions are in circulation**   See Varese, *Russian Mafia*, pp. 170–1.

27 **fictitious marriage**   Ivan'kov's 'American' wife was Irina Ola. She was paid $15,000. The marriage was arranged by the duo Elena and Leonard Lev. See James O. Finckenauer and Elin J. Waring, *Russian Mafia in America* (Northeastern University Press: Boston, MA 1998), p. 236.

28 **'At first, all we had was a name'**   Quoted from Friedman, *Red Mafiya*, p. 132.

28 **There is a red thread** See Friedman, *Red Mafiya*, pp. 132–3; Luke Harding, *Collusion* (Granta: London 2017), pp. 283–5.

29 **Russian clients** See again Harding, *Collusion*, p. 286.

29 **A report on crime** This material is available at https://www.nj.gov/sci/russians.shtm.

29–30 **the businessman Dmitrii Rybolovlev** See Federico Varese, 'Il Goldfinger russo con un tesoro artistico e uno strano legame con Trump', *La Stampa*, 17 November 2017, https://www.lastampa.it/topnews/tempi-moderni/2017/11/17/news/il-goldfinger-russo-con-un-tesoro-artistico-e-uno-strano-legame-con-trump-1.34386456, and Federico Varese, 'Asset management: On "Salvator Mundi" and the unreality of the art market', *Times Literary Supplement*, 14 August 2019, https://www.the-tls.co.uk/articles/salvator-mundi-da-vinci-art.

31 **an interview conducted from his prison for a Russian TV channel** The interview can be found at https://www.youtube.com/watch?v=LA1bW_DBruo.

31 **He died on 9 October 2009** See Michael Schwirtz, 'For a departed mobster, wreaths and roses but no tears', *New York Times*, 13 October 2009.

32 **His associates spared no expense** See Nikolai Syromyatnikov, 'Skol'ko stoili pokhorony Yaponchika?' ['How much did Yaponchik's funeral cost?'], *Ruskaya Semerka*, 18 December 2018, https://russian7.ru/post/assiriyskiy-zyat-zachem-mertvomu-vo; 'Vse pro pokhorony Yaponchika' ['Everything about Jap's funeral'], Mzk1.ru, 30 March 2020, https://www.mzk2.ru/2020/03/vse-pro-poxorony-yaponchika.

32 **The police arrested three people** They are Khaka Gazzayev, Murtazi Shadania, and Dzhambuk Dzhanashia (see *Kommersant'*, 13 December 2021) They got respectively 14-year, 15-year and 16-year jail sentences.

32 **In September 2023** See Elena Balayan, 'S doma vydachi

net: Gde skryvaetsya ot rossiiskogo suda odin iz ubiits Yaponchika' ['There is no extradition from the house: Where one of Yaponchik's killers is hiding from the Russian court'], *Izvestiya*, 27 September 2023, https://iz.ru/export/google/amp/1579672.

Notes to Chapter 2

34 **The architect of the privatization programme** For Philip Short, *Putin, His Life and Times* (Bodley Head: London 2022, p. 249), this was not a 'bribe' but rather a form of *mzdoimstvo*; and yet the common rendering of the old Russian word мздоимство is 'bribe'. See also Petr Aven, *Vremya Berezovskogo* [*Berezovsky's Era*] (OOO Izdatel'stvo AST: Moscow, 2018), pp. 357–8 and Klebnikov, *Godfather of the Kremlin*, p. 273.

35 *The View from the Kremlin* The book was published in English by HarperCollins in 1994.

35 **Boris Berezovsky, co-owner of a magazine** Valentin Yumashev was deputy director of *Ogonek* [*Spark*]. In due course – that is, in 1997–8 – Yumashev would become head of the presidential administration.

36 **'perfectly happy Soviet childhood'** See Hoffman, *Oligarchs*, p. 130. In this paragraph and the next I draw upon Hoffman's account (pp. 127–49).

36 **'a surprising place'** Hoffman, *Oligarchs*, pp. 130–1.

37 **'Half of the things he said'** Hoffman, *Oligarchs*, p. 132.

39 **nine hundred lives** Evgenii Snegov, 'Bitva pod "AvtoVAZom"': Kak bandity v 90-kh borolis' za kontrol' nad Tol'yatti' ['The battle of AvtoVAZ: How bandits fought for control of Togliatti in the '90s'], *Sekret Firmy* [*Firm's Secret*], 30 September 2021, https://secretmag.ru/criminal/bitva-pod-avtovazom-kak-bandity-v-90-kh-borolis-za-kontrol-nad-tolyatti.htm.

39 **Ivanov, founder and director** The newspaper

founded by Valerii Ivanov, which closed in 2014, was called *Tol'yattinskoe obozrenie* [*Tolyatti Review*].

42 **eighteen companies had been sold** The data on early 1990s privatization come from Maxim Boycko, Andrei Shleifer, and Robert W. Vishny, *Privatizing Russia* (MIT Press: Boston 1997).

42 **On 20 March Yeltsin declared emergency rule** Reddaway and Gilinsky, *Tragedy of Russia's Reforms*, p. 395.

42 **A presidential decree to dissolve parliament** Klebnikov, *Godfather of the Kremlin*, pp. 121–2.

43 **The number of victims** For estimates of how many deaths and injuries occurred during the events of 3 and 4 October 1994, I consulted https://ru.wikipedia.org/wiki/События_сентября_—_октября_1993_года_в_Москве. See also David Satter, 'Yeltsin: Shadow of a doubt', *National Interest*, 34 (1993–4), p. 52 and Enrico Franceschini, 'Nel Bunker in fiamme', *la Repubblica*, 5 October 1993.

43 **In a phone call from Air Force One** The phone call between Clinton and Yeltsin can be found in the National Security Archive at https://nsarchive.gwu.edu/document/30730-document-06-memorandum-telephone-conversation-telcon-president-boris-yeltsin-russian, under the title 'Memorandum of telephone conversation: Telecon with President Boris Yeltsin of Russian Federation, 5 October 1993. It is a declassified White House document available at the Clinton Digital Library.

44 **Scholars have questioned** Electoral fraud is discussed in Richard Sakwa, 'The Russian elections of December 1993', *Europe–Asia Studies*, 47(2), 1995, pp. 195–227, esp. 218–20. See also Matt Bivens, 'Ballot fraud: Not if, but how much', *Moscow Times*, 4 June 1996.

44 **Yuri Luzhkov** Quoted from Short, *Putin*, p. 211.

45 **Berezovsky threw himself headlong to ensure Yeltsin's**

re-election   See Mikhail V. Zygar, *Vse svobodny: Istoriya o tom, kak v 1996 godu v Rossii zakonchilis' vybory* [*Everyone Is Free: The Story of How Russia's 1996 Elections Ended*] (Alpina Pablisher: Moscow 2021).

45 **The head of the presidential guards concocted**   Short, *Putin*, p. 213; Leon Aron, *Yeltsin: A Revolutionary Life* (St Martin's Press: New York 2000), pp. 580–633.

45 **secret loans**   Short, *Putin*, p. 220. NTV was owned by Vladimir Gusinky.

45–6 **Vladimir Pozner**   Aven, *Vremya Berezovskogo*, p. 232.

47 **power vertical**   Short, *Putin*, p. 220. See also Gilles Favarel-Garrigues, *La verticale de la peur: Ordre et allége-ance en Russie poutinienne* (La Découverte: Paris 2023).

Notes to Chapter 3

The text of this chapter draws upon, and expands on, Federico Varese, 'Inferno russo', *la Repubblica*, 16 January 2022.

48 **one of the most significant and controversial documents**   See https://www.primecrime.ru/pho to/private/20049.

48 **Russian prison**   This description applies to remand prison (*sledstvenny izolyator*, SIZO), where individuals are held while awaiting trial, investigation, or sentenc-ing. Conditions in SIZOs are often harsh. Overcrowding is now pervasive in a minority of remand prisons in regional capitals and in Moscow. Most prisoners are held in correctional colonies, each with a different 'security regime' (strict, medium, minimum). Nowadays there is no overcrowding in correctional facilities. I am grateful to Judith Pallot for pointing this history out to me.

50 **Kolyma**   During the Soviet era, the Kolyma Gulag camps were located in the Dalstroi region of Russia. Dalstroi, an acronym for the Far North Construction Trust (in Russian), was a territory in the Russian Far East; and it was under its administration that the notori-ous Kolyma camps operated. These jails were part of

the Gulag system. To understand this crucial aspect of Russian and Soviet history, see the important studies by Judith Pallot – for instance 'The Gulag as the crucible of Russia's 21st-century system of punishment', *Kritika: Explorations in Russian and Eurasian History*, 16(3), 2015, pp. 681–710.

51 **Ivan Astashin** I interviewed Ivan Astashin, Olga Romanova, Sergei Savel'ev, and Vladimir Osechkin in January 2021. A very useful text by Ivan Astashin on the sexual rules in prison can be found at https://vk.com/@delo_abto-turmaikhui. In July 2022, Ivan began publishing excerpts from his book *Puteshestvie po mestam lisheniya* [*Journey to Places of Deprivation*] on the website of *Novaya Gazeta*, https://novayagazeta.ru/articles/2021/06/01/pu teshestvie-po-mestam-lisheniia.

54 **the quantity of the stolen material is extraordinary** Sergei's cache of videos was not the first to be smuggled out of the prison system. In 2018, webcam recordings of the beating of prisoner Makarov by eighteen officers in Yaroslavl correctional colony no. 1 were made public in *Novaya Gazeta*. Even the authorities had to admit that the footage was genuine. Before 2018, torture videos taken on mobile phones circulated widely, but were always declared fakes by authorities. Officers now have to record any use of physical force on a body cam, and this is why these official videos started 'escaping' colonies. I am grateful to Judith Pallot for pointing out this history to me.

55 **commented Olga Romanova** Irina Romaliiskaya, '"Putina rasstroili ne pytki, a utechka informatsii o nikh": Ol'ga Romanova: O prichine uvol'neniya glavy FSIN' ['"Putin was upset not by the torture, but by the leak of information about it": Olga Romanova: About the reason for the dismissal of the head of the FSIN'], *Current Time*, 26 November 2021, https://

www.currenttime.tv/a/olga-romanova-o-prichine-
uvolneniya-glavy-fsin/31579328.html.

55 *Proekt* **published a critical article** Katya Arenina,
with Mikhaila Rubina, 'Na doverii: Portret Vladimira
Osechkina, predprinimatelya ot pravozashchity' ['On
trust: Portrait of Vladimir Osechkin, human rights
entrepreneur'], *Proekt*, 11 September 2023, https://
www.proekt.media/portrait/vladimir-osechkin.

58 **A long article published in** *Novaya Gazeta* **on 15
December** Nikita Kondrat'ev, 'Unizhat' i glumit'sya ne
lyudskoe, mozhno tol'ko sochuvstvovat'' ['To humiliate
and mock is not human; one can only sympathize'], *Novaya
Gazeta*, 15 December 2021, https://novayagazeta.ru/artic
les/2021/12/15/unizhat-i-glumitsia-ne-liudskoe-mozhno
-tolko-sochuvstvovat?utm_source=fb&utm_medium=
novaya&utm_campaign=i-vot-kogda-ves-pytochnyy-
instrumentari.

58 **The analyses published on the MediaZona
website** Dima Shvets, 'Progon v pustotu: Pochemu tak
slozhno vyyasnit', pravda li vory v zakone reshili reabil-
itirovat' "opushchennykh po bespredelu"' ['"An edict into
the void: Why is it so difficult to find out whether thieves
in law really decided to rehabilitate those "thrown into
lawlessness"?'] MediaZona, 17 December 2021, https://
zona.media/article/2021/12/17/progon.

58 **Eva Merkacheva** See Saniya Yusupova, '"Nel'zya
ikh priravnivat' k petukham": Pomozhet li
"vorovskoi progon" zhertvam pytok v rossiiskikh
koloniyakh' ['"You can't equate them to roosters":
Will the "thieves' edict" help victims of torture in
Russian colonies?'] *Current Time*, 17 December 2021,
https://www.currenttime.tv/a/vorovskoy-progon
-zhertvy-pytok-kolonii/31611890.html.

59 **Dubai Declaration** Discussed in Varese, *Mafia Life*,
pp. 91–2.

60 **Criminal Code**   See Article 2010.1 of the Russian Criminal Code. The provision was first used in October 2020 at the trial of *vor* Shalva Ozmanov, known as Kuso, who got eleven years. Then, on 15 June 2023, *vor* Yurii Pichugin was sentenced to life. See 'V Moskve vpervye vynesli prigovor po stat'e o "vorakh v zakone": Kto takoi Shalva Ozmanov?' ['In Moscow, for the first time, a sentence was handed down under the article on "thieves in law": Who is Shalva Ozmanov?'], BBC Russian Service, 8 October 2020, https://www.bbc.com/russian/news-54462520; 'Sud prigovoril k pozhiznennomu vora v zakone i lidera "bandy Pichugina"' ['The court sentenced the thief in law and leader of the "Pichugin gang" to life'], RBC, 15 June 2023, https://www.rbc.ru/society/15/06/2023/648b35159a79478c0e84df10.

61 **From 2020, those who promote the culture of the 'criminal world'**   This is the ruling against the AUE (*arestantskii uklad edin*, 'prison order universal'). See e.g. 'Russia outlaws children's criminal underground movement', *Moscow Times*, 17 August 2020, https://www.themoscowtimes.com/2020/08/17/russia-outlaws-childrens-criminal-underground-movement-a71178. The same fate occurred to the LGBT+ movement in 2023. They are both considered extremist organizations, alongside the Islamic State and the Taliban. See Maria Chiara Franceschelli and Federico Varese, *La Russia che si ribella: Repressione e opposizione nel paese di Putin*. Milan: Altra Economia, 2024.

62 **the 'mafia-type criminal association' to be found in other criminal codes**   See Francesco Calderoni, 'A definition that does not work: The impact of the EU Framework Decision on the fight against organized crime', *Common Market Law Review*, 49(4), 2012, pp. 1365–93.

62 **Denis Golikov admitted that he was a torturer in the**

Irkutsk camp   Saniya Yusupova, 'Chto zhiv ostalsya – chudo: Pytki zaklyuchennykh v Priangare' ['It's a miracle that you're still alive: Torture of prisoners in the Angara region'], *Siberian Realities*, 11 October 2021. https://www.sibreal.org/a/chto-zhiv-ostalsya-chudo-pytki-zaklyuchennyh-v-priangare/31503147.html.

63 **Kseniya Sobchak** The recording of the 2021 end-of-the-year conference is available at https://www.1tv.ru/news/2021-12-23/418526-kseniya_sobchak_na_press_konferentsii_prezidenta_podnyala_vopros_o_pytkah_v_rossiyskih_tyurmah.

64 **add this note**   See https://pikabu.ru/story/vorovstvu_i_analnyim_orgiyam_8801594.

64 **'The typhoid quarantine'**   The story is included in Varlam Shalamov, *Kolyma Tales*, translated by John Glad (Penguin Books, London 1994), pp. 147–69.

Notes to Chapter 4

The text of this chapter draws upon (and expands) Federico Varese, 'Nikita e la rete di Gozi', *la Repubblica*, 9 September 2021. To write it, I consulted the following court documents:

- United States vs Nikita Vladimir Kuzmin, Sealed Complaint, 11 Cr 387 (LBS) November 29, 2010
- Preet Bharara, Gozi Virus Press Conference, 23 January 2013, transcript
- United States vs Mihai Ionut Paunescu, Sealed Complaint, 13 Crim 41, 2013
- United States vs Calovskis, US District Court, Southern District of New York, No. 12-cr-00487.

I also consulted the following reports and blogs:

- Group IB Reports
- Andrei Yakovlev, *The Dark Side of Russia*, IntSights Report, 2020
- Russia's Most Dangerous Cyber Threat Groups, IntSights Report, 2020

- Max Goncharov, *Russian Underground 2.0*, TrendLabs, 2015
- Krebs on Security Blog
- Kaspersky Lab
- European Cybercrime Centre, Report, 2014.

66 **stepfather's children**   The famous Russian singer Vladimir Kuzmin appears to have been Nikita's stepfather. At first Kuzmin confirmed that he was the adopted father ('Nikita has his own father, I just raised him', declared the singer in 2010), then denied it ('This is not my son, it's a mistake', he said in 2016). For the 2010 statement, see Irina Bobrova, 'Odna zvezda Vladimira Kuz'mina Populyarnyi rok-muzykant: "Pugacheva ne p'et, ya ne p'yu, chto zrya v gosti khodit"' ['The star Vladimir Kuzmin, popular rock musician: "Pugacheva doesn't drink, I don't drink, there's no point in visiting"'], *MK*, 30 May, 2010 (https://www.mk.ru/culture/interview/2010/05/30/500105-odna-zvezda-vladimira-kuzmina-foto.html). For the 2016 statement, see Daniel Turovskii, 'Psikh, Smelyi i drugie glavnye kiberprestupniki planety' ['Psycho, Brave and other top cybercriminals on the planet'], *Meduza*, 15 September 2017 (https://amp.meduza.io/feature/2017/09/15/psih-smelyy-i-drugie-glavnye-kiberprestupniki-planety).

67 **Today the system is made up**   See Jonathan Lusthaus, *Industry of Anonymity: Inside the Business of Cybercrime* (Harvard University Press: Boston, MA 2018).

67 **'there was also a manager who was paid $50,000 to $60,000 a year'**   Jonathan Lusthaus, Jaap van Oss, and Philipp Amann, 'The Gozi group: A criminal firm in cyberspace?', *European Journal of Criminology*, 20(5), 2023, p. 1707.

68 **'one of the most financially destructive computer viruses in history'**   Quoted from https://www.justice.gov/usao-sdny/pr/three-alleged-international-cyber-criminals-responsible-creating-and-distributing-virus.

68 **This type of virus continues to be the most requested one in criminal forums**   Data come from the 2020 IntSights report dedicated to Russian cybercrime.

69 **the team transitioned to full cybercrime-as-a-service mode**   I am grateful to Mauro Vignati for discussing this point with me.

72 **45,000 subscribers and reached an average of 1,300 comments per day**   See Andrei Yakovlev, *The Dark Side of Russia*, IntSights Report, 2020.

72 **120 thousand members**   Yakovlev, *Dark Side of Russia*.

72 **Max Goncharov**   See Max Goncharov, *Russian Underground 2.0*, TrendLabs, 2015.

73 **dentrino**   As quoted in Jonathan Lusthaus, 'Trust in the world of cybercrime', *Global Crime*, 13(2), 2012, p. 81.

77 **The picturesque town**   I visited the Romanian town of Râmnicu Vâlcea in 2015. See Federico Varese, 'Romania, nella tana degli hacker che truffano il mondo', *La Stampa*, 12 April 2015. For an academic study on the topic, see Jonathan Lusthaus and Federico Varese, 'Offline and local: The hidden face of cybercrime', *Policing: A Journal of Policy and Practice*, 15(1), 2021, pp. 4–14. It is important to note that the town is known for cyberfraud, not for hacking activity, hence 'Hackerville' can lead to misunderstandings.

79 **Vladimir Anikeev**   Vladimir Anikeev, the founder of Shaltai-Boltai, was released in 2018 and, according to some sources, cooperated with elements of the FSB. See Lincoln Pigman, 'Hacker who aided Russian intelligence is sentenced to 2 years', *New York Times*, 6 July 2017.

80 **A group of researchers**   The research group's experiments on how to inject doses of distrust into online criminal markets are partly reported in Lonie Sebagh, Jonathan Lusthaus, Edoardo Gallo, Federico Varese, and Sean Sirur, 'Cooperation and distrust in extra-legal networks: A research note on the experimental study

of marketplace disruption', *Global Crime*, 23(3), 2022, pp. 259–83.

81 **'there was such a tragedy here'**   Quoted from United States vs Nikita Vladimir Kuzmin, Sealed Complaint, 11 Cr 387 (LBS) November 29, 2010, p. 18.

81 **'audi was in the winter, the convertible in the summer'** Quoted from United States vs Nikita Vladimir Kuzmin, ibid.

81 **Trump's son in 2016**   Oliver Laughland, 'All the president's men's lawyers: Who are Trumpworld's leading attorneys?' *The Guardian*, 15 July 2017, https://www.theguardian.com/us-news/2017/jul/15/donald-trump-russia-lawyers-kasowitz-futerfas.

82 **Deniss Calovskis, the Gozi programmer, was captured in Latvia**   Nate Raymond, 'Latvian man spared more US prison time over Gozi computer virus', *Reuters*, 5 January 2016, https://www.reuters.com/article/idUS KBN0UJ247.

82 **attend an official Kremlin event**   An article published on Meduza on 15 September 2017 reports that Kuzmin attended an official Kremlin event while in prison in the US.

82 **was sentenced to three years in prison**   See Department of Justice, 'Romanian national who operated "bulletproof hosting" service that facilitated the distribution of destructive malware sentenced to three years in prison', 12 June 2023, https://www.justice.gov/usao-sdny/pr/romanian -national-who-operated-bulletproof-hosting-service- facilitated-distribution.

83 **CheckPoint   Research**   https://research.checkpoint .com/2020/gozi-the-malware-with-a-thousand-faces/ #:~:text=,Thousand%20Faces%0A%0A%20August%20 28%2C%202020.

Notes to Conclusions

84 **the cooperative movement**   A still useful early study of the cooperative movement in the 1980s is that of Anthony Jones and William Moskoff, *Ko-ops: The Rebirth of Entrepreneurship in the Soviet Union* (Indiana University Press: Bloomington 1991).

85 **the tumultuous 1990s**   In Russian, *likhie devyanostye*.

86 **Bullies and plunderers**   See Holmes, 'Lineages of the rule of law', p. 20.

86 **Anna Politkovskaya**   I wrote about the murder of this journalist in Federico Varese, 'L'omicidio di Anna Politkovskaja nella Russia di Putin', *Lo Straniero*, 77 (2006), pp. 12–14.

86 **1999 terrorist attacks**   The list of observers who believe the FSB is responsible for the bombings that took place in various Russian cities in 1999 is long and includes Pavel Voloshin, the reporter from *Novaya Gazeta*, Anna Politkovskaya, and Aleksandr Litvinenko. In agreement is also the authoritative study by the late John B. Dunlop, *The Moscow Bombings of September 1999: Examinations of Russian Terrorist Attacks at the Onset of Vladimir Putin's Rule* (Ibidem-Verlag: Stuttgart 2014). Dunlop names three key members of Yeltsin's inner circle as the originators of the plan. Two members of the investigative commission established by parliament have died in suspicious circumstances. The lawyer for the same commission was arrested for revealing state secrets. See David Satter, *The Less You Know, the Better You Sleep: Russia's Road to Terror and Dictatorship under Yeltsin and Putin* (Yale University Press: New Haven, CT 2016, pp. 1–39). 'It is hard to imagine that Berezovsky was not involved [in the bombings]', writes Satter (p. 28). Short (*Putin*, pp. 2–14) is among the sceptics.

87 **Surely Russia also modernized, at least until around 2012**   Data come from Treisman, *The New Autocracy*.

The American scholar Ronald Inglehart has documented how societies with high education, service-oriented economies, and significant exposure to information tend to develop demands for expression and participation, a strong intolerance for corruption, and requests for an efficient and fair state. The political scientist Daniel Treisman and his collaborators have demonstrated how the case of Russia in the twentieth century conforms to this model: there is nothing anomalous or surprising about it, contrary to those who argue for an ineffable and unique Russian soul. The percentage of those in favour of a democratic political system increased from 45 to 68 percent from 1995 to 2011. In 2012, 70 percent agreed that political opposition was necessary (compared to 47 percent in 2000), and public opinion was favourable to the European Union and the United States (70 per cent and 60 per cent respectively). For a general discussion on the relationship between democratization and development, see Ronald Inglehart and Christian Welzel, 'How development leads to democracy: What we know about modernization', *Foreign Affairs*, 88(2), 2009, pp. 33–49.

87 **GDP** GDP per capita is calculated by the World Bank for the period 1990–2020: https://ourworldindata.org/search ?q=GDP+per+capita+Russia. I take other data from Daniel Treisman (ed.), *The New Autocracy* (Brookings Institution Press: Washington, DC 2018), pp. 1–29 (Introduction).

87 **Indem** The Indem data are cited from Satter, *The Less You Know*, p. 81. The Corruption Perceptions Index referred to in the text is compiled by Transparency International.

87 **According to 2022 calculations** See Mark Galeotti, 'Times of Trouble: The Russian underworld since the Ukrainian invasion', Global Initiative Research Report, November 2023, p. 10.

87 **man 'with winter eyes'** The expression 'winter eyes' (зимние глаза) is used by Aleksandr Herzen (Aleksándr Gértsen) to describe Tsar Nicholas I; see his memoir *Byloe i Dumy* [*My Past and Thoughts*] (Eksmo: Moscow 2007 [1870]), p. 34.

88 **media manipulation** See Sergei Guriev and Daniel Treisman, *Spin Dictators: The Changing Face of Tyranny in the 21st Century* (Princeton University Press: Princeton, NJ 2022).

88 **'geopolitical catastrophe'** As quoted in Short, *Putin*, p. 408 and n. 220, p. 781.

88 **Andrei Klishas** As quoted in Giovanni Boggero, 'La mobilitazione mostra che la parola di Putin vale più della legge', *Il Foglio*, 20 December 2022, https://www.ilfoglio.it/esteri/2022/12/20/news/la-mobilitazione-mostra-che-la-parola-di-putin-vale-piu-della-legge-4778897. Boggero is quoting in turn from an article by Evgeniya Kuznecova published in the 8 December issue of the Russian newspaper *Vedomosti*.

89 **motivated by domestic repression** The argument that military interventions in Ukraine are a function of domestic political considerations and, above all, the fear that the Ukrainian example could infect Russia have been expressed, among others, by Service, *Kremlin Winter* and by Aleksei Navalny, 'How to punish Putin', *New York Times*, 20 March 2014. See also Federico Varese, 'Se la democrazia spaventa lo Zar', *la Repubblica*, 7 March 2022.

89 **NATO expansion** On Putin's instrumental use of the NATO aggression thesis, see Robert Person and Michael McFaul, 'What Putin fears most', *Journal of Democracy*, 22 February 2022, https://www.journalofdemocracy.org/what-putin-fears-most.

89 **Hannah Arendt** Quotations are from Hannah Arendt, *The Origins of Totalitarianism* (George Allen & Unwin: London 1951), p. 323.

89 **Ioann Burdin**   I interview Burdin in Federico Varese, 'Ribellione russa: Le voci dell'opposizione alla guerra di Putin in Ucraina', *la Repubblica*, 17 March 2022. See also Maria Chiara Franceschelli and Federico Varese, *La Russia che si Ribella* (Altra Economia: Milan 2024), pp. 23–32.

90 **The war in Ukraine in 2022 may have additional unintended effects that lead to weakening the system**   I make these points in Federico Varese, 'Ucraina, le mani della mafia sulla guerra: Se i conflitti diventano un trampolino per i clan', *la Repubblica*, 29 March 2022 and 'La guerra in Ucraina fa la gioia degli hacker e della mafia russa (che Putin si vantava di aver estirpato)', *l'Espresso*, 5 September 2022.

91 **Stockbrokers interviewed by Bloomberg**   See Varese, 'La guerra in Ucraiana'.

91 **Even in Russia observers**   Anna Pereverzeva, '"Likhie 90-e": Vozvrashchenie?' ['Are "the wild '90s" returning?'] https://www.sovsekretno.ru/articles/obshchestvo/likhie-90-e-vozvrashchenie100723; also referenced in Galeotti, 'Times of Trouble', p. 39.

91 **Sanctions imposed**   See e.g. Alexander Kupatadze and Erica Marat, 'Under the radar: How Russia outmanoeuvres western sanctions with help from its neighbours', Research Paper No. 18, University of Birmingham, 2023; Galeotti, 'Times of Trouble', p. 28. The theft of Ukrainian grain epitomizes the criminalization of the shipping industry.

91 **Several friends of mine**   See Federico Varese, 'La scelta di Nikolaj: "Tangenti, ossa rotte così chi non va via prova a salvarsi"', *la Repubblica*, 24 September 2022.

92 **people trained in the use of violence**   For Sicily, see Diego Gambetta, *The Sicilian Mafia* (Harvard University Press: Boston, MA 1993); for Russia, Federico Varese, 'Is Sicily the future of Russia? Private protection and the

rise of the Russian Mafia', *European Journal of Sociology/ Archives Européennes de Sociologie*, 35(2), 1994, pp. 224–58.

92 **Some directly recruited from prison**   See Judith Pallot, 'Lies, damn lies and statistics: How many prisoners has Wagner really recruited?' *Riddle*, 7 March 2023, https://ridl.io/lies-damn-lies-and-statistics-how-many-prisoners-has-wagner-really-recruited.

92 **crimes involving firearms**   Crimes involving firearms increased by 30 per cent in 2022 according to Ministry of Internal Affairs (MVD) data cited in Galeotti, 'Times of Trouble', p. 18.

92 **myriad of associations**   This is a point made by Mark Galeotti in a webinar on 18 December 2023.